NEGLIGENCE IN HEALTHCARE

A simple guide for patients, carers and practitioners

Marc Cornock & Andy Nichols

Straightforward Publishing
www.straightforwardbooks.co.uk

Straightforward Guides

© Marc Cornock and Andy Nichols, First Edition, 2024

Marc Cornock and Andy Nichols have asserted the moral right to be identified as the authors of this work. Under the Copyright, Designs and Patents Act 1988

All rights reserved. No part of this publication may be reproduced in a retrieval system or transmitted by any means, electronic or mechanical, photocopying or otherwise, without the prior permission of the copyright holder.

British cataloguing in Publication Data. A catalogue record for this book is available from the British Library.

ISBN 978-1-80236-316-6

Printed by 4edge www.4edge.co.uk
Typesetting by Frabjous Books
Cover design by BW Studio Derby

Whilst every effort has been made to ensure that the information contained within this book at the time of going to press, the authors and publishers cannot accept liability for any errors and omissions contained within, or for any changes in the law since publication.

To Caroline and Damian,
for all the help and assistance,
and for the loan of the 'garret'.
My thanks, Marc

With thanks to my wife for tolerating me,
Andy

CONTENTS

CONTENTS v
PREFACE.. xiii
ABOUT THE AUTHORS xv
ACKNOWLEDGEMENTS xvi
LIST OF LEGISLATION AND CASES xvii
    Legislation xvii
    Cases.. xvii

INTRODUCTION 1
    Focus of this book.. 1
    Approach to writing and presentation 2
        A brief note on terms and terminology................................ 3
        Discussing legislation and cases... 5
    Structure of the book.. 5
        List of legislation and cases 6
        An analogy (Chapter 1) 6
        Overview of the law and sources of law (Chapter 2)............ 6
        What is negligence? (Chapter 3) 7
        Duty of care (Chapter 4)... 8
        Breach of duty and the standard of care (Chapter 5) 8
        Harm (Chapter 6)... 9
        Causation (Chapter 7).. 10
        Defences (Chapter 8) 11
        Damages (Chapter 9) 11
        Revisiting the milk float (Chapter 10) 11
        Reference list... 12
        Glossary 12
        Resources... 12
    Index.. 12

1 MILK FLOATS AND NEGLIGENCE 13
Why an analogy? 13
The analogy in action 14

2 OVERVIEW OF THE LAW AND SOURCES OF LAW 17
Legal jurisdictions 18
Legal interest or not? 19
What is the law? 20
    Some examples of rules 20
    The law as rules 20
    The milk float and laws 21
    Types of punishment 23
Where does law come from? 23
    Legislation 24
    Cases – common law 25
    The doctrine of precedent 27
    Hierarchy of courts 28
Legislation vs common law 31
Civil and criminal cases 31
    Which court 32
    Who brings and investigates the case 32
    Witnesses 32
    Burden of proof 33
    Standard of proof 33
    Case names 34
    Summary of a negligence case 34
Summary of Chapter 2 35

3 WHAT IS NEGLIGENCE? 36
Definitions of negligence 37
Negligence as a type of law 38
Tort 39
    Notes on tort 43
Ginger beer and a snail 44
    The facts of the case 44

CONTENTS

Possible legal actions Mrs Donoghue could pursue 45
Mrs Donoghue's legal action 49
The legal principle established in Donoghue v Stevenson
   [1932] 50
Summary of the Donoghue v Stevenson [1932] case 51
The tort of negligence in healthcare 52
The purpose of negligence in healthcare 53
The elements (or wheels) of negligence in healthcare 56
Summary of chapter 3 58

4 DUTY OF CARE 61
What is a duty of care? 61
Why is it important to consider when a duty of care exists? 62
When does a duty of care exist? 63
   The neighbour principle revisited 63
   A development in establishing the duty of care 64
   The Caparo 3 stage test 66
   An example of the lack of proximity in a legal case
      examining a medical issue 68
   Proximity and public policy 70
   Special relationships 71
Who is the duty of care owed to? 72
Liability 77
   A healthcare practitioner's areas of accountability
      liability 78
Liability issues 81
   Vicarious liability 81
   Acting in the course of employment 84
   The liability of students 88
   Indemnity 88
   Team liability 90
   Delegation and liability 92
Good Samaritan acts 93
Summary of chapter 4 97

5 BREACH OF DUTY AND THE STANDARD OF CARE 99
Breach of duty 100
    What is a breach of the duty of care? 100
The general standard of care 103
The standard of care in healthcare 107
    Bolam and reasonableness 109
    Bolam and responsibleness 113
    Expert witnesses 115
Developments since the establishment of the Bolam test 117
    Introducing an element of logic into the 'Bolam test' 120
    A qualified 'Bolam test' 123
    A modification on the 'Bolam test' 124
Evidence based practice 126
Keeping up to date 127
Policies & guidelines 129
Emergencies and the standard of care 131
    Emergencies within a healthcare environment 131
    Emergencies outside a healthcare environment 133
The standard for juniors and trainees/students 134
Advanced Practitioners: the standard for specialist
or special skills 137
A team standard? 140
Summary of chapter 5 141

6 HARM 145
Harm as the third wheel of the milk float 146
Forms of harm 147
    Death 148
    Negligence before birth 148
    Physical injury 149
    Psychiatric injury 150
    Pain and suffering 152
    Loss of chance 152
    Wrongful birth 153
    Wrongful life 154

CONTENTS

Gross negligence manslaughter..155
Summary of chapter 6 157

7 CAUSATION 158
Proving causation 159
    Burden and standard of proof.. 159
    Omission rather than a positive act 160
    The two tests of causation 161
    Res ipsa loquitur 161
The first test: factual causation 162
    Material contribution to the harm 165
    Intervening acts... 166
The second test: legal causation 167
    Novus actus interveniens revisited................................... 168
    Eggshell skull rule.. 169
Summary of chapter 7 169

8 DEFENCES 171
Defences in legal cases 171
Defences available in cases of negligence in healthcare 172
    Mistaken identity 173
    Dispute over the facts 173
    The wheels have come off the milk float.........................174
    Novus actus interveniens...176
    Contributory negligence 176
    Volenti non fit injuria... 178
    Statutory limitation 179
Summary of chapter 8 181

9 DAMAGES 183
What are damages?.. 183
Terminology of damages 184
The award of damages 186
    How is the award of damages made?................................ 187

Heads of damages 190
    Special and general damages.. 191
    Specific heads of damages 191
How damages are calculated 194
When damages may be reduced..197
    Contributory negligence 197
    Costs of making a claim 198
    Interim payments... 198
    State benefits 198
    NHS charges... 199
Summary of chapter 9 200

10 REVISITING THE MILK FLOAT.. 201
    The milk float revisited.. 201
    Milk float deliveries and making a claim of negligence
        in healthcare..203
        Frivolous and fraudulent claims.......................................204
        Motivation of patients who pursue legal claims 206
    Alternatives to making a legal claim of negligence
        in healthcare 207
        Complaints...208
        The Parliamentary and Health Service Ombudsman 209
        Patient associations/support organisations 210
        Healthcare regulatory bodies... 211
        Alternative dispute resolution 212
        Final point and resources 215
    The financial cost of negligence in healthcare........................215
    The process of making a claim of negligence in
        healthcare 217
    Consequences of negligence in healthcare............................220
        Effects on those involved in a claim................................ 221
        Effects on those not involved in a claim 222
        Effect on healthcare practice 223
    Summary of chapter 10 225

x

CONTENTS

REFERENCES 227
GLOSSARY OF NEGLIGENCE RELATED TERMS 229
RESOURCES 238
    For patients 238
    Support for healthcare practitioners 239
    Law and sources of law.. 239
    Courts 240
    Parliament websites 240
    Ways to raise concerns about healthcare, healthcare
        practitioners and the legal profession 241
        NHS complaints services 241
        Websites of the healthcare regulatory bodies 241
    General 242

INDEX 243

PREFACE

When we started thinking about writing a book on negligence in healthcare we were aware that there are many, many books written about clinical negligence, that is negligence that relates to a clinical situation. Indeed, we have read most of these books during our time teaching negligence to students and practitioners. However, there are two reasons why we believe it was necessary for us to write this book and add one to the total number of books on negligence.

The first reason was that negligence can be a very difficult concept to understand when you first come across it. Generally, you need a guiding hand to help you through the concept. Most books written about clinical negligence are written either for lawyers who practise in that area of law or for law students. These can be quite difficult to read without prior knowledge of the legal system, legal conventions and how the law works. The other audience for clinical negligence is healthcare practitioners, although there are some good books written with them in mind, most of the available literature for them is written as a chapter in a larger book on law and ethics applied to healthcare and can therefore be quite superficial.

This leads us to the second reason behind the writing of this book. We believe that the information that patients, carers and healthcare practitioners need in relation to negligence in healthcare is the same. The patient and the carer both need to know what standard of care they should expect to receive and whether particular care has fallen below the standard to amount to negligence. Additionally, the practitioner needs to know what standard they need to achieve when providing care to patients, and how their practice is assessed. All three groups need to understand the legal principles of negligence and how this applies to healthcare.

Therefore, it is our aim that this book can be used by several different audiences: patients, those individuals who are currently interacting with healthcare practitioners; relatives and carers of those who are receiving care and/or treatment; healthcare practitioners and student healthcare practitioners who provide the care and treatment to the rest of us; and finally, those with an interest in healthcare law, in particular negligence in healthcare practice.

We have written this book from the assumption that readers will not have any prior knowledge of healthcare law. The book includes all the areas necessary for each of the different audiences, yet we have kept the content as short as possible. Likewise, we have only included as much detail as is necessary to make the various points and approached the writing to make it accessible to all our intended audiences. This, we trust, will make the subject more user-friendly.

A little caveat: the information in this book is not to be taken as legal advice, rather it is an explanation and discussion of the legal principles that relate to negligence in healthcare practice.

Marc & Andy

ABOUT THE AUTHORS

Marc Cornock is a Senior Lecturer in Healthcare Law at The Open University. He worked as a healthcare practitioner before moving into the education of healthcare practitioners. His interest in healthcare law developed during his time as a practitioner. Marc teaches and writes about healthcare law and how it affects practitioners and patients.

Marc has also written:

- Marc Cornock (2021) *Key Questions in Healthcare Law and Ethics* Sage
- Marc Cornock (2023) *Accountability and Professionalism in Nursing and Healthcare* Sage
- Marc Cornock (2023) *Consent: A Pocket Guide for Nursing and Health Care* Lantern Publishing
- Marc Cornock & Lindsay Giddings (2023) *Healthcare Rights and law for patients, carers and practitioners* Straightforward Publishing
- Marc Cornock (2023) *Confidentiality: A Pocket Guide for Nursing and Health Care* Lantern Publishing

Andy Nichols is a Lecturer in Nursing at Plymouth University. His background is in communicable disease control and public health and his interest in healthcare law developed during his time practicing in public health. Andy has written and published on a number of topics and has a particular interest in interprofessional learning and teaching in healthcare law.

Andy & Marc used to teach law together, to healthcare students at the University of Plymouth

ACKNOWLEDGEMENTS

Andy & Marc would like to acknowledge the many students and colleagues they have taught and worked with over the years who have contributed to their understanding of healthcare law.

Additionally, Marc would like to say thank you to his friends and family who put up with him during his writing. The biggest thanks go to Sarah, without whom he would never get started, or finished.

LIST OF LEGISLATION AND CASES

Legislation
page
Congenital Disabilities (Civil Liabilities) Act 1976 149
Law Reform (Contributory Negligence) Act 1945 177
Limitation Act 1980 179
Social Action, Responsibility and Heroism Act 2015 94

Cases
Barnett v Chelsea & Kensington Hospital Management
Committee [1968], 1 All ER 1068 .... 74–76, 164
Blyth v Birmingham Water Works Co. (1856) All ER
[1843–60] 478 .... 37, 104
Bolam v Friern Hospital Management Committee [1957] 2
All ER 118 109–125
Bolitho v City & Hackney Health Authority [1997] 4
ALL ER 771 .... 120, 125, 160
Caparo Industries plc v Dickman and others [1990] 1
All ER 668 .... 64, 65, 70, 95
Cassidy v Ministry of Health [1951] 2 KB 343 83
Century Insurance Co. Ltd v Northern Ireland Road Transport
Board [1942] 1 ALL ER 491 86
Cork v Kirby MacLean Ltd [1952] 2 All ER 402 .... 163, 178
Cowley v Cheshire and Merseyside Strategic Health Authority
(2007) 94 BMLR 29 131
Donoghue v Stevenson [1932] All ER 1 .... 44–51, 63, 64, 72

F v West Berkshire Health Authority [1989] 2 All ER 545 93

Goodwill v British Pregnancy Advisory Service [1996]
2 All ER 161 68

Gregg v Scott [2005] 4 All ER 812 153

Hall v Brooklands Auto-Racing Club [1932] All ER 208 105

Iqbal v London Transport Executive [1973] EWCA Civ 3 87

Jones v Manchester Corporation [1952] 2 QB 852 134

Limpus v London General Omnibus Co. (1863) All ER
[1861–73] 556 ....84, 85

McFarlane v Tayside Health Board [1999] 4 All ER 961 153

McKay v Essex Area Health Authority [1982] 2 All ER 771 154

McKew v Holland & Hannen & Cubitts (Scotland) Ltd. [1969]
3 All ER 1621 166

Maynard v West Midlands Regional Health Authority
[1985] 1 All ER 635 .... 119, 125, 138

Nettleship v Weston [1971] 3 All ER 581 135

Overseas Tankship (U.K.) Ltd v Morts Dock and Engineering
Co Ltd [1961] 1 All ER 404 167

Pearce v United Bristol Healthcare NHS Trust (1998)
48 BMLR 118 125

R v Adomako [1994] 3 All ER 79 155

Roe v Ministry of Health [1954] 2 All ER 131 .... 102, 115

Storey v Ashton [1869] LR 4 QB 476 85

Sutherland Shire Council v Heyman (1985) 60 ALR 65

Wilsher v Essex Area Health Authority [1986]
3 All ER 801 .... 90, 132, 138, 140

INTRODUCTION

This introduction serves three purposes: it allows us to outline the focus of the book, it gives an insight into the approach we have taken to the writing and presentation of the book, and finally, by providing a brief description of each chapter we can outline the book's structure.

Focus of this book

Our focus in writing this book has been to discuss negligence in relation to healthcare events and healthcare practice. We will discuss the definition of what negligence is in chapter 3. For now, we can say that this book is concerned with the acts, care and treatment, that are undertaken by healthcare practitioners for patients. In particular whether these acts meet the expected standard, how this can be assessed and what a patient or carer can do if the standard is not met. We will also be discussing omissions of care and treatment.

In a nutshell, the focus of *Negligence in healthcare: A simple guide for patients, carers and practitioners* is the legal duty that health practitioners have to their patients, and what options are available to patients and carers if this legal duty is not met.

As you will probably have realised from the book's title, we are focusing on negligence within healthcare. This is negligence that occurs when healthcare practitioners are caring for or treating patients or when they should be caring for or treating patients. We are not limiting our discussion of negligence to that which occurs in formal healthcare settings because a considerable proportion of healthcare is provided outside of formal healthcare settings, such as in patient's homes.

One final point to say about the focus of this book. We are discussing negligence in healthcare from the perspectives of the patient, and their carer(s), and that of the healthcare practitioner. This means that at times we will discuss an incident from three perspectives. This allows us to consider what the patient may need to prove to establish negligence has occurred but also what the healthcare practitioner needs to prove to show that their actions were not negligent.

Approach to writing and presentation

The main point we would like to make about our approach to the writing and presentation of this book is that we have adopted a conversational style. There are times when we need to discuss some detailed concepts and principles, however we have endeavoured to do so as if we and you were in a room, and we could discuss this together as if we would if were able to have a conversation.

We have not adopted a conversational tone because we consider negligence in healthcare to be a frivolous topic or one that we do not take seriously. Indeed, our conversational approach to writing is actually because of the opposite. We are both passionate about our teaching and both believe that it is vital that patients and healthcare practitioners understand the rights that patients have and also that understanding the principles of healthcare law can lead to more effective practice by healthcare practitioners.

Our approach to the writing and presentation of this book has been led by our teaching practice where we know that our students prefer to learn in a less formal way (we know because they tell us!).

INTRODUCTION

We have occasionally included some information as 'an aside', this is because they are not a vital part of the discussion regarding negligence in healthcare but explain an aspect of law that is either interesting, to us at least, or provide background context to a point that is being made.

A brief note on terms and terminology

It was recognised in Marc's previous book (*Healthcare rights and law for patients, carers and practitioners 2023*) that in law and healthcare some terms and terminology that are used can be problematic when seen out of context. Also, that terms and terminology from a previous era can be offensive and/or seen as patronising when read today.

Our aim with this book is to be informative and to assist you in understanding this area of law and healthcare. Neither of us wants to offend anyone and we certainly recognise that if we offended you, you would probably stop reading and this would defeat our aim.

That said, to fully explain and discuss the principles of negligence in healthcare we need to refer to laws and legal cases which originated in a previous age where the terms and words used are not the ones we would use today. We have kept our use of what may be offensive or patronising wording and terminology to a minimum. However, please note that when a word that you consider is or could be offensive and/or patronising we would ask you to recognise that we are using that word or term because it is in the original and not because we agree with its use in that particular way.

In a similar way, it wasn't until 2007 that a change was made so that gender-neutral language was to be used in the drafting and writing of legislation. This means that for legislation prior to this date excerpts from legislation, and also from policies and legal cases, you will see reference to 'he' and 'him' rather than gender neutral terms. We will use the original terms used, not to be exclusionary or outdated but because these are the words that were used, and we want to present the original arguments used in legal cases and the actual definitions and concepts in legislation.

When we discuss legislation and cases that does not use gender neutral terms please accept that masculine should include the feminine and vice versa, unless we state otherwise.

So, in summary, we have used gender neutral language in our writing unless we are referring to a source that uses gendered terms and terminology when we will use that too for that specific purpose.

A final point on terms we have used in our writing. When we use the following words the definitions here are the way that we are using them:

Patient
We use this to mean someone who is interacting with healthcare practitioners and may be receiving healthcare care and/or treatment or expecting to receive care and/or treatment. We use the term patient to include client. We also use patient to mean an adult or child.

Healthcare practitioner
We use this term to mean someone whose occupation is to provide care and treatment to patients. It includes all those who have a role with patients. We are using this term so that we do not need to list each and every type of healthcare practitioner each time we want to discuss something. Examples of healthcare practitioner include chiropodists, dental hygienists and nurses, dieticians, doctors, midwives, nurses, occupational therapists,

paramedics, physiotherapists, radiographers, and speech therapists.

We also use the term to include anyone who is a student training to be a healthcare practitioner.

Discussing legislation and cases

We will be using shortened case names within the chapters of the book. The full case names will be in the list of legislation and cases at the beginning of the book, and, where we have quoted from them, also in the reference list at the end of the book.

The full names are provided in case you should wish to look up individual cases for yourself. However, when we introduce and discuss a piece of legislation or a case, we will provide a brief outline of the relevant part of the legislation or the facts and outcome of the case. So, you should not need to look up the cases in order to follow our discussion of them.

Not all the legislation or cases that we will be discussing and using to illustrate the various aspects of negligence in healthcare will necessarily be healthcare related themselves. This is because legal principles apply to all similar legal issues, regardless of the area that the facts of the case originate from.

Structure of the book

This book is about negligence in healthcare. That is negligence that occurs during the care and treatment of a patient, or when a patient should be being cared for and/or treated.

Negligence in healthcare is a subject that is an aspect of law and legal processes. Thus, to fully explore negligence in healthcare we need to discuss the law and the legal system as it relates to negligence in healthcare.

As the law and legal system underpins negligence in healthcare we have structured the book so that the underpinning aspect of law and the legal system comes before we discuss the actualities of negligence in healthcare, and what negligence is and what needs to be established to prove a case of negligence in a court of law.

The remaining part of this section outlines the order in which we have discussed all the various aspects of negligence in healthcare, including the underpinning aspects related to the law.

We have used the introductions to each of the chapters to describe the order in which we are discussing the various aspects of negligence in healthcare. Providing the introduction to each of the chapters here, will allow you to see where we discuss each of the aspects, as well as seeing what comes before and after a specific aspect of the discussion. Together with the index this should allow you to locate a specific aspect of the discussion and go straight to it.

So, without further ado, the structure of the book is as follows:

List of legislation and cases

An analogy (Chapter 1)

This chapter has one aim, to introduce you to an analogy that you can use to aid your reading of the chapters that follow. The analogy we are using is that of the milk float.

Overview of the law and sources of law (Chapter 2)

This chapter provides an overview of law and the legal system, because negligence in healthcare is based upon legal principles. We have included the chapter because we are not assuming that you have any prior experience of studying law and so the aim of the chapter is to help ensure that the legal information in the chapters that follow are more readily understood. The chapter is not an in-depth review of the law but rather the aspects of law that are relevant to negligence in healthcare. Essentially, the basics that we believe you will need to fully engage with in the subsequent chapters.

The chapters that follow chapter 2 discuss legal principles, predominantly from legal cases, to explore negligence in healthcare and what has to be established for negligence to be proved. If you have a good understanding of law, the legal process and sources of law then feel free to skip past this chapter.

Chapter 2 examines what law is and the two main ways in which law originates. It discusses the legal system and the two main legal systems, including the hierarchy of the courts, in England and Wales. It concludes by looking at how a civil and a criminal legal case may proceed through the legal system.

What is negligence? (Chapter 3)

The focus of this chapter is concerned with discussing negligence through addressing what the legal concept of negligence is and what the purpose of having negligence as a legal option is.

The chapter begins with a definition of negligence, before seeing where negligence is positioned into the overall legal landscape by asking what type of law negligence is. This requires a discussion of the type of laws that exist and identifying negligence as a form of tort law. In this discussion tort law is differentiated from other forms of law by examining what tort is and what the purpose of tort law is.

Following this we explore how negligence has evolved from the earlier definition and what the modern concept of negligence is. This discussion involves us discussing a legal case from 1932 that was concerned with ginger beer and snails. This 1932 case is explored because it can be said to be the case that changed negligence into what we know today. The discussion of this legal case study also allows us to illustrate various points about negligence and how a case is brought.

Once we have digested the 1932 case we move on to consider negligence in healthcare and ask what the difference is between general negligence and negligence in healthcare. We also discuss what the purpose of negligence in healthcare is. Chapter 3 ends by asking what a person bringing an action for negligence in healthcare needs to prove to be successful in their case.

Duty of care (Chapter 4)

In this chapter we examine the duty of care element of negligence in healthcare. As part of this examination, we consider what a duty of care is and why establishing a duty of care is important in making a claim for negligence in healthcare. This leads us into a discussion on when a duty of care exists in relation to healthcare and who the duty of care is owed to. Following this discussion, we examine liability and what this means and the types of liability that can exist, along with considering specific issues that arise in the liability of healthcare practitioners. Finally, we look at the duty of care in relation to Good Samaritan acts by healthcare practitioners.

Specifically, chapter 4 will answer the question of when a duty of care exists between a healthcare practitioner and a patient.

Breach of duty and the standard of care (Chapter 5)

Chapter 5 is concerned with breaches of the duty of care. This will involve a discussion of what breach of the duty of care means, the standard by which any alleged breach can be judged and whether there is a specific standard for cases of negligence in healthcare.

INTRODUCTION

As part of the discussion assessing whether a breach of care has occurred the role of expert witnesses in negligence in healthcare cases will be examined.

Following the discussion on breach of the duty of care and the required standard of care there is an exploration of how the standard of care is applied in specific circumstances: such as in emergencies; within healthcare teams; when the healthcare practitioner is a student or otherwise inexperienced; or is an advanced healthcare practitioner; whether there is a team standard for those healthcare practitioners who work as part of a defined team; and how any of these may affect the standard of care and the assessment of whether the duty of care has been breached.

Consideration is also given in chapter 5 to the emergence of evidence-based practice, how up to date a healthcare practitioner needs to be, and the role of policies and guidelines on the practice of healthcare practitioners.

Harm (Chapter 6)

This is a relatively short chapter, not because proving harm has occurred is not an important part of a negligence in healthcare claim, it is in fact vital, but because harm is unique because people and their bodies are unique. Two identical negligent actions can result in two very different forms of harm in different individuals. Harm must therefore be judged as a question of fact on a case-by-case basis. The court will decide either that harm has occurred or it has not.

In many cases, whether harm has occurred or not is not an issue, or at least not a complex issue, because it is a matter of fact. If a surgeon cuts the wrong leg off a patient that the leg was cut off is a fact. The issue would be more about the causation of the harm and what damages to pay to the patient.

However, these are issues for chapters 7 (causation) and 9 (damages).

One issue with regard to harm is whether the harm that the patient has suffered is a type of harm that can be claimed for in a case of negligence in healthcare.

Therefore, chapter 6 will briefly look at what harm is, what forms of harm are recoverable and, acknowledging that the most severe form of harm that could happen is the death of the patient, this chapter also examines gross negligence manslaughter.

Causation (Chapter 7)

Chapter 7 represents the fourth wheel of the milk float which is taking our case of negligence in healthcare forward. The first, second and third wheels did their job of establishing that a duty of care was owed in chapter 4, that the standard of care was breached in chapter 5, and that harm was suffered as discussed in chapter 6.

In this chapter we discuss how a patient who sues a healthcare practitioner for negligence in healthcare can prove that it was the actions of the healthcare practitioner that did in fact cause the harm that they have suffered.

There are several legal factors that need to be considered before a claimant can be said to have proved that the defendant's action caused them harm. These factors will include 'passing' both a factual test and a legal test and demonstrating that nothing stepped in the way of the healthcare practitioner's actions, and so disrupted the chain of causation.

This chapter will discuss both causation tests and the chain of causation. As well as other legal factors, including the eggshell skull principle.

INTRODUCTION

Defences (Chapter 8)

There are several defences that are available to a defendant who is defending their practice in a case involving negligence in healthcare. Therefore, the focus of chapter 8 is on the ways that a healthcare practitioner may defend a claim against them of negligence in healthcare.

Damages (Chapter 9)

This chapter is concerned with the award that is made at the end of a successful claim of negligence in healthcare by a patient. It begins by examining what damages are and what the purpose of them is. It then proceeds to look at the award of damages, including how damages are paid and the types of damages that are payable.

Following this there is an examination of how damages are calculated. Finally, we discuss what may reduce the amount of damages paid.

Revisiting the milk float (Chapter 10)

As the final chapter, chapter 10 revisits the analogy we have used to discuss negligence in healthcare, that of the milk float. After this revisit of the milk float, chapter 10 moves on to examine why a patient chooses to drive a milk float, that is the reasons why patients make a claim of negligence in healthcare against healthcare practitioners. This leads into a discussion of the alternatives to milk floats, or the alternatives to pursuing a legal claim that are available to patients.

The financial cost of milk floats, that is the financial cost of negligence in healthcare within the National Health Service is explored before considering how a milk float is driven or the process of making a claim for negligence in healthcare.

Chapter 10 ends by looking at the effects of the milk float on its driver and those it drives past, that is the effects of negligence in healthcare.

Reference list

Glossary

Although we define terms that are specific to our discussion when we first use them, we have included a glossary in case you want to check what a term means and are not sure where it was first defined.

Resources

The resources section contains a number of resources that may be useful to you if you wish to undertake further reading around negligence in healthcare, or about the law in general.

Index

There is an index at the end of the book to assist you with finding something specific.

CHAPTER 1

MILK FLOATS AND NEGLIGENCE

Okay, we both accept that this is a rather an odd title for a chapter in a book discussing negligence in healthcare but please bear with us.

This chapter has one aim, to introduce you to an analogy that you can use to aid your reading of the chapters that follow. The analogy we are using is that of the milk float.

Why an analogy?

Whilst we both believe that we are effective lecturers, according to our students anyway, we have realised how difficult it can be to grasp a concept like negligence on first discussing it, if you are not familiar with the law and legal process. Most of our students are healthcare students, that is individuals who were studying and training to be the healthcare practitioners of the future. They generally have no particular interest in the law save as it affects their healthcare practice.

There are also a lot of misconceptions about negligence that our students may have heard and which we needed to dispel. Many of these misconceptions are confusing because they link negligence with bad practice. So that if a nurse or a paramedic, or any other healthcare practitioner, were to be bad at their role this would be labelled negligence.

As you will see, this is not necessarily the case. Whilst negligence may involve a healthcare practitioner being bad or poor at their role, that in itself would not mean they have been negligent. Negligence is a way of determining if a healthcare practitioner's standard of care and/or treatment has been below standard. This is achieved through a consideration of various factors that all have to be proved for a negligence case brought by a patient to succeed.

What was needed was a way of demonstrating to our students that negligence was a systematic process where certain things had to be proved. That a healthcare practitioner merely being bad, or incompetent, was not sufficient for the healthcare practitioner's actions to be deemed as negligent.

As a result of this, Andy first came up with the analogy of the milk float as a way of explaining negligence to students. Although it sounds bizarre it really does help to understand negligence in healthcare. Chapter 3 will discuss what negligence is in more detail, but in chapter 1 we just want to take you through the analogy so that you have a framework to work with as you proceed through the book.

Just for clarity, when we talk about a milk float, we are thinking about the electric vehicles that were used to deliver milk to the front doors of our parents houses early each morning when we were both younger, a lot younger in Marc's case!

The analogy in action

Now let us discuss the title of this chapter and show you how a milk float is an analogy for negligence.

The milk float analogy works like this:

1. MILK FLOATS AND NEGLIGENCE

- milk floats move slowly and are incapable of moving fast – the same as the civil legal process where negligence in healthcare is dealt with
- there is a steering wheel that is used to set the direction of travel – a legal case involving negligence is driven to determine whether there was any fault
- milk floats have four wheels (originally they had three but thankfully there was an increase to four, or the analogy would not work!) – there are four things that need to be determined to prove a case of negligence
- wheel 1 = duty of care
- wheel 2 = was there a breach of the duty?
- wheel 3 = did any harm occur?
- wheel 4 = did the breach cause the harm?
- the spare wheel = time – there are limitations on when a case for negligence can be brought
- applying the brake stops the milk float going forward, this is the same as raising a valid defence
- milk floats carry milk, in crates. When they leave the milk depot the crates contain bottles full of milk and when they come back they are full of empty bottles. The amount of milk being caried = the amount of damages that are awarded
- if a wheel comes off the milk float, all the milk moves around and can come off the milk float. If one of the things that the wheels represents is not proved the case is lost, and no damages are paid, similar to the milk being lost. Additionally, there is only a limited supply of milk that can be carried and this equates to the total amount of damages that can be claimed or received
- as well as milk being carried, milk floats also carry non-milk products, this is similar to the two types of damages that may be payable – general and special damages

Please do not worry if this does not make full sense to you at the moment. By the end of this book, it should/will. For the moment just consider that for a case of negligence in a healthcare setting to be proved there has to be a milk float with four wheels being steered in a given direction, travelling with milk and possibly non-milk products, all moving rather slowly, and it has to deliver the milk to you.

Each of the individual aspects of the milk float (that is aspects of negligence) will be discussed in the chapters that follow.

If the milk float analogy is not one that works for you feel free to ignore it. It is not something that we are going to talk about a lot. We will come back to it at the end of the book to raise it once more and highlight how the analogy works again but otherwise it is just a vehicle, excuse the pun, for getting us started on discussing negligence in healthcare.

Chapter 2 is now going to leave the milk float analogy and provide an overview of the law and how laws originate.

CHAPTER 2

OVERVIEW OF THE LAW AND SOURCES OF LAW

This chapter provides an overview of law and the legal system because negligence in healthcare is based upon legal principles. We recognise that legal terminology and processes are not always transparent and accessible, therefore we have included the chapter because we are not assuming that you have any prior experience of studying law and so the aim of the chapter is to help ensure that the legal information in the chapters that follow are more readily understood. The chapter is not an in-depth review of the law but rather the aspects of law that are relevant to negligence in healthcare. Essentially, the basics that we believe you will need to fully engage with in the subsequent chapters.

The chapters that follow chapter 2 discuss legal principles, predominantly from legal cases, to explore negligence in healthcare and what has to be established for negligence to be proved. If you have a good understanding of law, the legal process and sources of law then feel free to skip past this chapter.

Chapter 2 examines what law is and the two main ways in which law originates. It discusses the legal system and the two main legal systems, including the hierarchy of the courts, in England and Wales. It concludes by looking at how a civil and a criminal legal case may proceed through the legal system.

Legal jurisdictions

A jurisdiction is an entity (for instance, a country or nation or a nation state) that has been legally established and has its own legal system and is able to make its own laws. There are four separate jurisdictions in the United Kingdom. These are England, Northern Ireland, Scotland, and Wales. Some laws cover the whole of the United Kingdom, some only apply to one jurisdiction and others apply to two or more jurisdictions.

Because of the existence of separate legal jurisdictions around the world, we feel that it is important to point out that legislation (legislation is defined below) that exists in one jurisdiction does not necessarily apply in a different jurisdiction. As you will see later in this chapter, jurisdictions have the right to pass their own legislation and it is only the legislation that they pass that have effect in that jurisdiction.

With regard to case law (this is also defined below), a case will generally only apply in the jurisdiction where the case was heard. Therefore, it does not automatically apply in other jurisdictions. However, where there is similarity in the laws that exist in different jurisdictions the judgment in a case heard in jurisdiction A may have relevance in jurisdiction B and so the judgment in the case may be persuasive for cases in jurisdiction B that are based on similar facts and legal issues as the original case.

What this means in practice is that legislation and cases are generally jurisdiction specific and so when we look at the laws that exist, we refer only to the laws within that jurisdiction.

Because of the differences in the laws and the way that the legal systems operate in the various jurisdictions within the United Kingdom, we will be dealing with the law as it applies to the jurisdiction of England and Wales as they share the

2. OVERVIEW OF THE LAW AND SOURCES OF LAW

same legal justice systems and also have the same laws relating to negligence in healthcare. However, the overall principles discussed within this book can be taken to apply throughout the United Kingdom.

Legal interest or not?

If we generalise, we can say that there are three types of people when it comes to being interested in the law. These being:

- those who have an interest in the law and how it works, such as Andy and Marc;
- those who are ambivalent about the law; and
- those who are disinterested in the law and would rather do anything else than read about the law and legal processes

We assume that, as you are reading this book, you have at least a passing interest in the law and legal process. However, if you fall into either of the last two groups we hope that we can welcome you into those of us who have an interest in the law.

Regardless of what group you feel you fall into, and especially if you are in one of the latter two groups at the moment, we would like to reassure you that you do not need to know or remember all that follows in this chapter in a lot of detail. Rather you need an overview so that you can understand how laws arise and how the legal process works.

Just one final word before we move on to consider the law itself, we are providing you with this information so that in the chapters that follow, when we talk about negligence and the effect that a legal case has had on an aspect of negligence, the legal aspects are not a distraction.

What is the law?

It is very common to talk about the law, as in the law says this, or the law doesn't let you do that, or what an ass the law is. But when we talk about the law what actually are we talking about?

The law is about rules. Rules are something we all live by, whether it is our own personal rules, the rules of our family or those of our employers. Rules are all around us. Rules allow us to all live together in relative harmony, at least when the rules are followed and if the rules are not contradictory.

Some examples of rules

As an example, we, Andy and Marc, have rules about writing this book. These rules relate to who does what and when certain tasks have to be done. The idea behind these rules is that both of us know what aspect of the book we are responsible for and when it needs to be done. This creates harmony between us as it means that we don't both do the same task and we know that everything is taken care of and the book will be complete, so long as we follow the rules we have set ourselves.

We both work in universities, albeit different ones at present. We use our work e-mail systems to share the drafts of the chapters we have written. To be able to do this we each have to abide by our respective organisation's rules on the use of e-mail, especially the rules about downloading attachments from outside of our organisations. The reason for these rules is to protect our employer's IT system from being compromised.

The law as rules

In the two examples just given, the rules relate to a limited group or groups of individuals. The rules we have set ourselves for the writing of this book only affect the two of us. Possibly also, to

2. OVERVIEW OF THE LAW AND SOURCES OF LAW

a limited extent, our publisher as if we do not follow them we may miss our publishing deadline and the book would either not get published or would be published late.

The rules relating to the use of e-mail from our employers only affect employees of our respective organisations. However, it is considered important that some rules are followed by everyone, in that they are seen as special rules. These special rules apply to everyone and if someone does not follow them they can be punished. This is what a law is: a rule that is considered to be so important that it has been given special meaning and a penalty is attached to it if it is not followed to encourage us all to follow it. With a law, as opposed to a rule, the authority of society through the legal processes that exist within that society are used to enforce compliance with the law.

That is what a law is, and the law as a whole is the sum total of all the rules that have been given special status (all the individual laws) and the mechanism by which those laws can be enforced.

The milk float and laws

To illustrate the concept of laws and their effect, let's consider the milk float and what laws exist that relate to it.

The milk floats leave the depot driven by the milkman carrying milk to be delivered to its customers. It delivers these products to individual households and picks up empty milk bottles to be returned to the depot.

Several rules can be seen in the act of a milkman using a milk float to deliver milk to their customers:

- the milkman is driving the milk float and so needs to comply with any rules relating to driving
- the milk float is being driven on public roads and so needs to comply with traffic rules

- the milk float is a vehicle and so need to comply with rules relating to road tax
- the milk float is carrying a number of milk crates, each with a certain number of bottles of milk. If you remember milk floats of old you will recall that they were rather noisy as all the milk crates used to move about and the milk bottles clattered against each other. There are rules about producing noise during certain hours of the day/night
- the milkman may need to take rest breaks. There are rules relating to the amount of rest an employee is entitled to during a shift they work
- the milk that is delivered to households has to be paid for. There are rules about paying for goods you received, as well as the rules that a company will have about how payment is made and how frequently payment should be made
- as well as delivering milk, the milkman also collects the empty milk bottles that households leave out for them. There may be company rules about whether the milk bottles have to be clean before they can be collected for return to the depot

All this illustrates that many activities that we may take for granted can be subject to numerous rules. Further, that some of these rules are actually laws and as such have a punishment attached to them if they are not followed.

In the example of the milk float the laws include the rules about driving and using public roads. Some of the penalties that could be imposed for breach of these rules include the milkman being fined for, say, speeding, although unlikely in an old-fashioned milk float. More likely the milkman would be fined for parking on double yellow lines or nowadays using their mobile phone whilst driving. In addition to the fine the milkman would most

2. OVERVIEW OF THE LAW AND SOURCES OF LAW

likely receive penalty points on their driving license which will increase the cost of their insurance, whether for them personally or for their company insurance policy.

Types of punishment

The form of the punishment that can be given if a law is not followed will depend upon the type of law.

Generally, a civil legal matter will have a 'punishment', usually referred to as a remedy in civil matters that requires the person who loses to pay a monetary award to the person who is successful in their case. Although other remedies can include the terms of a contract being adhered to, or the person who loses their case having to abide by certain restrictions such as not contacting a particular person.

The punishments, usually called a sentence in a criminal matter, for not following a criminal law include:

- being fined
- being subject to the requirements of a community order, for instance a curfew, having to undertake unpaid work, and/or having to attend rehabilitation courses
- being sent to prison

Where does law come from?

Different countries have different ways of establishing the laws within their own countries but in the United Kingdom there are two main ways that laws originate:

- legislation
- cases or common law

As a generalisation, legislation is used to set the overall direction of the law of a country and case law is used to settle disputes between individuals.

Legislation

There are several terms used to describe legislation, these include statutes, Acts, primary legislation, and secondary legislation. Apart for the last, they all refer to the same thing, laws that originate from Parliament or its equivalent, and are written down in one document. By Parliament or its equivalent we mean: the Westminster Parliament which can make law for the whole of the United Kingdom or for various parts of the United Kingdom; the Scottish parliament; the Northern Ireland Assembly and the Senedd or Welsh Parliament, (formerly known as the National Assembly of Wales). The laws made by Scottish Parliament and the Northern Ireland Assembly and the Senedd only apply to their respective countries and not to the whole of the United Kingdom.

An example of legislation is the Road Traffic Act 1988 which lays down the laws that our milkman has to adhere to when he is using the milk float to make the milk deliveries.

Secondary legislation is slightly different as it refers to laws that are made for parliament but not by parliament. Parliament sets out the requirements and the boundaries for the law, but it is made by another body. This is why secondary legislation is often called delegated legislation as parliament has delegated the authority to make the legislation to another body. These other bodies include government departments such as the Department of Health and Social Care.

Delegated legislation is differentiated from other legislation by usually having the word Order or Regulation or Rule in its title.

Legislation can be used in several ways:

2. OVERVIEW OF THE LAW AND SOURCES OF LAW

- to create a new law
- to amend an existing law to make it more relevant to the current time
- to repeal a law that is no longer needed
- to consolidate several laws into one place
- to confirm what the law is on a particular issue or to clarify a legal position, this is generally used when case law has resulted in an area of uncertainty

Although legislation will have a year in its title that does not mean that it is in force at that time. Most legislation will have a date written within it when it comes into force or will note that another piece of legislation, usually secondary legislation, will set the date for its commencement. Additionally, unless it specifically states so in the particular piece of legislation, legislation does not go out of date and has to be repealed to be cancelled and not be applicable anymore.

If you are interested in how a law is made in parliament there is a link in the resources area that you can use.

Cases – common law

Although legislation is the chief source of law in the United Kingdom it is not the sole source of law. Law in the United Kingdom is a combination of legislation and case law.

Law that is made through cases heard in courts is usually known as common law. Sometimes law that arises through legal cases is referred to as judge-made law. However, this is based on an incorrect assumption that judges, in making their decisions in these legal cases, are actually making law.

The way that common law actually works is that a judge or judges in a particular case will give their judgment on the facts that are presented to them, and their interpretation of the law applied to those facts. The judgment they give is the 'result' for that particular case. This is the end of the case, unless there is an appeal against the judgment.

The mechanism by which a judgment in one case can become part of the law is that the judgment does not just say that one side has won and the other lost. Rather, the judgment is a summary of the arguments presented and they provide a lot of discussion as to what law is relevant to which set of facts. The judge(s) then go on to give their outcome along with a discussion of how they reached that decision along with reference to the relevant law.

Thus, there is a lot of information in a judgment as to how a decision was reached and what law(s) were considered by the judge(s) in reaching their decision.

All judgments in court cases are recorded. This means that it is possible to go and see the reasons why a particular judgment was reached.

Along with recorded judgments, the second part of the operation of common law is a principle known as the doctrine of precedent. The doctrine of precedent is based upon a hierarchical structure to the court system and is related to the authority that one court has over another. The higher a court is in the court structure, the more authority it has.

The role of the courts is to apply the law in the case they hear. Where the law is unclear, they interpret the legislation that exists to provide a judgment for the particular facts of the case they are hearing. If there is no legislation that exists, they will look to other legislation that can be considered similar to see if anything can be extrapolated to cover the facts before them. In either situation, if there is no legislation that adequately provides a basis for a judgment, they will consider other legal cases where the same or similar facts have been considered and use the judgment in those cases to make their judgment.

The doctrine of precedent

The doctrine of precedent works as follows:

Court A hears a case concerned with a legal issue and issues a judgment on this.

Court B then hears a case with similar facts as Court A and the same legal issue. Depending upon the hierarchical position between Court A and Court B, Court B may either have to follow the judgment by Court A (known as binding precedent) or may have to give serious consideration to the judgment from Court A in making its own judgment (known as persuasive precedent), or Court B may be entitled to consider the judgment from Court A as irrelevant to the case it is hearing.

The difference between a binding and a persuasive precedent is that a binding precedent has to be followed, so the courts that hear later cases have to apply the same legal principles in the same way, whereas persuasive precedent gives some discretion to the later courts hearing cases on the same legal issues as to how they apply the precedent. This means that they can depart from the precedent if there is a legal reason to do so.

Precedent may be deemed to be irrelevant because it arose from a court that is lower in the hierarchy to the court now hearing a case, or because the legal issue in the current case is different to the one in the earlier case, or because the facts of the case are substantially different meaning that a different application of the law is required.

Precedent is the way that common law 'makes' law. Although legislation is paramount to common law, legislation may be unclear on a particular point that was either not considered when the legislation was enacted, or the situation has changed so that the legislation is no longer relevant on a particular point. There is also the situation where there is no legislation on a particular issue. It is then that common law applies.

A case that has binding precedence is often referring to as a leading case. What is a leading case changes over time as new laws are applied to similar sets of facts, this will be apparent when we discuss the various elements that have to be proved in negligence cases in subsequent chapters.

Hierarchy of courts

There are two separate but related legal justice systems that operate within the United Kingdom. These are the civil and the criminal legal justice systems. The civil justice legal system primarily deals with legal issues between individuals or between companies or organisations or any combination of these. The criminal justice legal system deals with prosecuting those who are said to have breached the criminal law.

Sometimes one legal issue will result in an issue having to go through both legal justice systems. This occurs with negligence in healthcare, and we will consider this in chapter 6 when we discuss gross negligence manslaughter. However, we will primarily be dealing with the civil justice system in our discussion of negligence in healthcare.

Each of the legal justice systems has its own court structure and so its own hierarchy of courts. Although at the top of the hierarchy there is a common structure.

At the top of the hierarchy in both the civil and criminal court hierarchy is the United Kingdom Supreme Court. It is sometimes referred to as the 'highest court of the land' because of this. It only hears cases that arise from the Court of Appeal and

2. OVERVIEW OF THE LAW AND SOURCES OF LAW

extremely rarely from the High Court. It only agrees to hear an appeal where the case involves an important legal principle or issue that needs deciding.

Next in the hierarchy for both the civil and criminal court hierarchy is the Court of Appeal, although there is a separate division for civil and criminal matters. So that there is a Court of Appeal (Civil Division) and Court of Appeal (Criminal Division). Regardless of the division, the Court of Appeal only hears appeals from courts lower in their respective hierarchies.

It is at this point in the hierarchy that the two legal justice systems have an entirely separate court structure.

In the criminal justice system, the next court would be the High Court and then below this Magistrates' Courts. The Crown Court is probably the court that most people would describe if asked. It hears criminal cases and has a judge and a jury, although a judge can hear cases without a jury in certain circumstances. It also hears appeals from magistrates court.

The Magistrates' Courts are the lowest level courts in the criminal justice system. They deal with some civil law but predominately hear criminal matters. They hear most criminal cases – over 90% of all criminal cases are decided at the Magistrates' Courts. To illustrate this, for the period January to December 2022 (the latest year for which complete figures are available) there were 91,657 completed Crown Court hearings, whilst in the Magistrates' Courts there were 1,266,297 completed court hearings. Generally, Magistrates' Courts deal with less serious offences but hear all bail applications apart from murder cases and refer cases to the Crown Court. Magistrates are not legally trained and are volunteers. Usually there is a bench of three magistrates for each case, although courts can sit with two magistrates. For more complex cases a District Judge can sit in a Magistrates' Court.

In the civil justice system, the court below the Court of Appeal (Civil Division) is the High Court. The High Court has three divisions: the King's Bench Division, the Chancery Division and the Family Division. All three divisions deal with high importance and high value civil cases. The High Court also has a supervisory function over all the courts below it.

The King's Bench Division deals with cases relating to contract and tort (for an explanation of tort see chapter 3). Thus, a case involving negligence in healthcare that was legally important or of high value would likely be heard in the King's Bench Division of the High Court. It also hears cases which question the decisions of the government (known as judicial review applications).

The Chancery Division deals with issues involving wills and bankruptcy, and issues relating to businesses, property and land. The Family Division hears the more important cases involving family matters including divorce and those matters that relate to children. The Family Division also hears appeals from the Family court.

Below the High Court is the County Court. It is the lowest court in the civil justice system and hears non-criminal cases where an individual or an organisation such as a business believes that there has been an infringement of their rights by another person or organisation.

Other courts in the civil justice system include:
- the Court of Protection which hears cases relating to individuals who lack the capacity to make their own decisions;
- the Family Court which hears most cases involving family matters including divorce and those matters that relate to children, except those that need to be heard in the Chancery Division of the High Court;

2. OVERVIEW OF THE LAW AND SOURCES OF LAW

- Coroners' Courts which make decisions on deaths that are considered to be unnatural or where the cause of death is unknown;
- Tribunals, such as employment tribunals

Legislation vs common law

Legislation can change the common law, but it is not possible for common law to change legislation. What this means is that legislation can be enacted which alters the legal principles the courts have to use but common law cannot overrule legislation or change the wording of legislation.

The only way that legislation can be changed is if it is repealed or if a later statute is enacted which changes the wording in the original statute.

The reason behind this is that legislation has primacy over common law, if there is a difference between the two it is legislation that should be followed. It is for parliament to decide if a law needs to be changed.

The aim of having legislation as the primary source of law is that legislation originates from parliament, and it is a recognition that it is parliament that has been given law making powers.

Civil and criminal cases

Both civil and criminal legal cases follow the same procedures as each other and are adversarial in nature. However, there are some differences between civil and criminal cases.

A brief aside: despite what you have seen on television and in films, the judges in United Kingdom courts in the do not use gavels, ever. The idea that gavels are used in courts in the

United Kingdom appears to have originated from seeing judges in American legal dramas using them.

Which court

Obviously, the court where the case is heard is different according to whether it is a civil or a criminal case, and the list of courts which hear each type of case is described in the 'hierarchy of courts'.

Who brings and investigates the case

With a criminal case it is the police who have a duty to investigate and the Criminal Prosecution Service who make the decision as to whether to bring the case to trial. Whereas in a civil case is it is the individual or organisation who has to decide to take a case to court and it is their legal team who will undertake any necessary investigation.

Witnesses

Most legal cases will involve witnesses. A witness may be called by either side and whichever side asks for the witness to attend, the other side will have an opportunity to ask questions of them and to question the evidence they are presenting.

There are two main types of witness:

Ordinary witness or witness of fact – someone who witnesses an event e.g. an assault or sees a patient receiving their care. Their role is to provide the facts.

Expert witness – someone who provides an opinion based on the facts using their clinical knowledge and expertise. They are often called by one side or the other, but they will give evidence to the court, and they are expected to be impartial and to give a reasoned opinion.

2. OVERVIEW OF THE LAW AND SOURCES OF LAW

Burden of proof

This means who has to prove their case.

In a criminal case the prosecution has to prove their case.

In a civil case, it is the person who brings the case (known as the claimant) who has to prove it.

In each type of case the defendant, the person who the case is against, does not have to prove anything and will win if the prosecution or claimant has not proved their case against the defendant.

Standard of proof

This refers to the standard that has to be reached for the prosecution or claimant to be considered to have proved their case.

In criminal cases the standard is higher than in civil cases. This is because in a criminal case the outcome could mean that the defendant on being found guilty is sentenced to imprisonment, and so loses their liberty. Whereas in a civil case the consequences of having a case found against them is not as serious and so means a lower level of standard of proof can be utilised.

The criminal standard of proof is 'beyond a reasonable doubt'. The judge or jury must be certain of the defendant's guilt before they can find them guilty. In reality, this means in all certainty it is considered that X happened, and it is the defendant who was the one who did X.

The lower standard of proof in civil cases is 'on the balance of probabilities'. This does not mean that is has to be beyond all reasonable doubt. Rather, in reality, this means that a judge is more convinced of one side's account than the other's.

Case names

The convention for case names is that the party bringing the case goes first, followed by v and then the name of the defendant(s).

Criminal cases usually start with R for Rex or Regina, as cases are brought in the name of the monarch. Sometimes a case will be named for the Crown Prosecution Service and so the case name will start with CPS not R. So, if a criminal case were being brought against Marc the case name would be R v Cornock or CPS v Cornock.

In a civil case it is the name of the person who is bringing the case, then 'v', and then the name of the defendant(s). Therefore, if Marc were bringing a civil claim against Andy the case name would be Cornock v Nichols.

In a criminal case the 'v' is read as 'against' and in a civil case it is read as 'and'. In neither case is the 'v' read out as 'versus'.

Summary of a negligence case

Assuming that Marc believes that he has suffered harm as a result of Andy's actions, and he has the necessary motivation, he could bring a case of negligence against Andy to seek a remedy for the harm he has suffered.

A case being brought to court alleging negligence in healthcare would be taken to the County Court or the High Court depending upon its legal or monetary importance.

It would be called claimant's name v defendant's name, if Marc brought his case against Andy it would thus be called Cornock v Nichols.

In this example the burden of proof would be upon Marc, as the person bringing the case. The standard of proof would be on the balance of probabilities, meaning does the judge consider

Marc's case to be more convincing than Andy's. If so then Marc wins the case, if not then Andy wins.

At the end of the case one party will have been successful in proving their case, assuming it is Marc he will receive a remedy from the court for the harm caused by Andy. The remedy will be in the form of an award of damages.

Summary of Chapter 2

Chapter 2 has examined legal jurisdictions, what law is, by reference to rules and how to ensure that rules are followed through the imposition of a penalty for not following a rule, and the types of punishment that can be applied to breaching different types of law. The chapter then considered legalisation and case or common law.

Considering common law involved a discussion of precedent and the court structure in the United Kingdom including the hierarchy of courts. Finally, chapter 2 noted the differences between civil and criminal cases.

All of this was to lay the foundations for the discussion which follows in the forthcoming chapters. The next chapter will provide a more detailed discussion around the law specific to negligence by answering the question, what is negligence?

CHAPTER 3

WHAT IS NEGLIGENCE?

The focus of this chapter is concerned with discussing negligence through addressing what the legal concept of negligence is and what the purpose of having negligence as a legal option is.

The chapter begins with a definition of negligence, before seeing where negligence is positioned within the overall legal landscape by asking what type of law negligence is. This requires a discussion of the types of law that exist and identifying negligence as a form of tort law. In this discussion tort law is differentiated from other forms of law by examining what tort is and what the purpose of tort law is.

Following this we explore how negligence has evolved from earlier definitions and what the modern concept of negligence is. This discussion involves us discussing a legal case from 1932 that was concerned with ginger beer and snails. This 1932 case is explored because it can be said to be the case that changed negligence into what we know today. The discussion of this legal case study also allows us to illustrate various points about negligence and how a case is brought.

Once we have digested the 1932 case, we move on to consider negligence in healthcare and ask what the difference is between general negligence and negligence in healthcare. We also discuss what the purpose of negligence in healthcare is. Chapter 3 ends by asking what a person bringing an action for negligence in healthcare needs to prove to be successful in their case.

3. WHAT IS NEGLIGENCE?

Definitions of negligence

Marc quite likes definitions; he finds that they give him a starting point upon which to organise his thinking on a particular subject. So, for his benefit, if not yours, we are going to look at an everyday definition of negligence and then a legal definition to start our discussion of what negligence in healthcare is.

According to the Shorter Oxford English Dictionary negligence is the *'lack of attention to what ought to be done; failure to take proper or necessary care of a thing or person; lack of necessary or reasonable care in doing something; carelessness* (Stevenson 2007).

Whilst, as we will see, the modern concept of negligence arose in a legal case from 1932, negligence is actually much older than that. One of the earliest standard legal definitions of negligence arose in a case from 1856 which concerned whether a water company laying water pipes correctly could foresee that an extreme weather event would result in ice build-up within a pipe that would in turn cause water to escape into a customer's property. In that case negligence was defined as *'the omission to do something which a reasonable man, guided upon these considerations which ordinarily relate the conduct of human affairs, would do, or doing something which a prudent and reasonable man would not do'* (per Alderson B. in Blyth v Birmingham Water Works Co. (1856) at page 479 -80). As the water company did everything that a reasonable company would have done, and the weather event was not a normal occurrence, they were found not to be negligent.

Although the language is very different, there are similarities between the two definitions and it is possible to say that, based on these definitions, negligence is about not doing something in the way that it would be expected to be done, or omitting to do something that it is expected would be done.

That said there are two ways in which lawyers use the word negligence. The first is along the lines of the definition just given. That is to use the word as a way of describing when someone does something, or does not do something, that results in harm to another person. This use of the word negligence is related to the duty that is owed by one person to another not to harm them through their actions or omissions.

The second way in which lawyers use the word negligence is in relation to the process whereby a person who has suffered harm as a result of someone else's actions or omissions can claim redress of that harm through the legal system. It is the way of receiving a monetary award for harm that has occurred as a result of a civil wrong.

Therefore, negligence is both an act and a process. It is based on the legal premise that if you cause harm to someone you should remedy that harm.

Now that we have a basic definition of what negligence is, it is time to locate negligence within the legal landscape and to determine why it is necessary to have negligence as a legal option: that is, what the purpose of negligence is.

Negligence as a type of law

Before we locate negligence within the law and outline what type of law negligence is, it is worthwhile discussing the different areas of law that currently exist.

The main areas of law are:

- contract law
- constitutional law/administrative law
- criminal law
- equity & trusts

3. WHAT IS NEGLIGENCE?

- land/property law
- tort

In chapter 2, *Overview of the law and sources of law*, it was noted that there are two legal justice systems, the civil legal justice system and the criminal legal justice system. Apart from criminal law, all the others predominately form part of the civil justice system. Although it must be noted, and we will come back to this when we consider harm in chapter 6, that even though the area of law that an issue falls under is a civil matter the actual legal issue that is in dispute can be a matter for both the civil and criminal legal justice systems.

It was also noted in chapter 2 that negligence in healthcare is a matter that falls within the civil legal justice system. This means that negligence is an aspect of civil law, specifically tort law. It fact, negligence is often referred to as the tort of negligence.

Tort

The word tort comes from the Latin 'tortus' which means twisted. Although it has also been said to originate from the French 'torde' which also means twisted. Whichever, root of the word you prefer, tort refers to something being twisted or not straight. That is something that is out of line with the norm, something that can in fact be thought of as being wrong.

Tort is an extremely complex area of law that has a myriad of rules, some of which can seem obscure and have so many exceptions to them it can make you wonder if the rule is ever followed. However, at its simplest, tort has one function and that is concerned with redressing wrongs that have occurred.

For a tort to exist, one person has to have committed a wrong, done something, that causes harm (what constitutes harm is discussed in chapter 6) to another person. There are various

types of tort, including:
- battery
- false imprisonment
- negligence
- nuisance
- personal injury
- trespass, to person or property

Negligence is said to be the most frequent form of civil action that is brought by a claimant.

In keeping with the discussion above regarding legal issues that can result in an action in both the civil and criminal legal justice systems, several of the torts noted above can be seen to have a possible criminal element to them as well having an action under tort law.

As a simple example of something having both a criminal and a tort element to them let's examine a nurse who gives an injection to a competent adult patient without their consent. For this example, all you need to know about consent is that without consent a competent adult patient cannot be treated. Therefore, the nurse cannot give an injection without the patient's consent and by doing so has committed a criminal act, most likely the crime of 'actual bodily harm'. If the patient were to report the nurse to the police they could be prosecuted for this in the criminal courts.

At the same time, as the patient has suffered harm they could, independently of the criminal charge, sue the nurse for the tort of battery, which is unlawfully touching someone, and seek redress for the harm they have suffered. The harm being the injection of the substance in the syringe. It is unlikely that the tort would proceed to court, unless the injection caused some serious consequences for the patient, but the example shows

3. WHAT IS NEGLIGENCE?

how one action can result in both a crime and a tort being committed.

It may be simplest to think of the civil and criminal elements of a single act as the tort of negligence being used to rectify the harm that has occurred, and the criminal law being used where a healthcare practitioner has intentionally caused harm to the patient.

As an aside, the crimes of assault and battery may not be what you think. Assault as a crime refers to threatened violence and battery as a crime is the actual violent act. Therefore, if one person were to threaten to punch another person and then did actually punch that other person, the threat to punch constitutes the crime of assault and the actual punch constitutes the crime of battery. Threatening to punch and then punching someone would be the combined crime of assault and battery. Battery is sometimes referred to as the execution of the threat in the assault.

Although, as just seen, an action by an individual can result in both a crime and a tort being committed, tort is primarily a civil legal matter. If someone wishes to pursue a claim for any of them, the first course of action would be in tort in the civil courts.

Because many of our students have confused the tort of negligence with breach of contract (obviously before we have taught them the law of negligence!), we would point out that tort and breach of contract are two entirely different areas of law and not variations of the same legal area. A breach of contract, not unexpectedly, is resolved using the legal principles of contract law not those of tort. A tort is a wrong that does not arise out of a contract.

Once a person has committed the wrong to another person, resulting in some form of harm, the tort is said to have been committed. Once a tort has been committed, the role of the law, that is tort law, is to ensure that person who committed the tort on the other person is legally liable to that other person for that tort and has to put right the harm that the other person has suffered.

Putting right the harm that occurs as a result of a tort is known as the remedy. Sometimes it is not possible to put right the harm that has occurred as a result of the tort and in these instances the remedy will be a monetary award that is made for the harm the person has suffered.

Other remedies available under tort law are injunctions to prevent an individual from committing an action that will cause harm to someone else, and expelling someone who is trespassing or otherwise unlawfully occupying someone else's property.

The overall aim of tort law is to put the person who has suffered the harm back to the position they were in prior to the tort being committed. However, as noted above, it is not always possible to put someone back in the position they would have been prior to the tort being committed. This is particularly so with cases of negligence in healthcare.

Taking a tort case against someone is known as bringing an action for tort. In relation to negligence in healthcare it would come under the tort of negligence and thus would be known as an action for negligence.

Most of the remedies that are available for a claimant who successfully brings an action for tort are common law remedies. This means that there is not a statutory remedy for the tort but rather the court hearing the action will decide the remedy based upon the doctrine of precedent and what has happened in other cases where the same tort with similar facts has been decided.

3. WHAT IS NEGLIGENCE?

Tort is therefore often referred to as a common law form of law and to discuss negligence, which as we now know, is a type of tort, it is necessary to discuss legal cases to determine the legal principles which have arisen as precedent.

Notes on tort

Before we move on discuss the tort of negligence, specifically negligence in healthcare, this section is a brief summary of tort.

Tort law is concerned with wrongs, civil wrongs.

There are various types of tort but regardless of the type of tort, the basis of tort law is to redress civil wrongs. That is the outcome of an action for tort is to put someone back in the position they would have been in had the tort not occurred.

Tort law only deals with civil wrongs.

Criminal acts are dealt with under criminal law in the criminal legal justice system.

Where an action can result in both a criminal charge and an action for tort, these would be pursued separately. The state prosecutes the criminal aspect, and an individual would bring the action for tort in the civil legal justice system.

To bring an action for tort, the person bringing the action has to have suffered some form of harm as a result of the tortious act.

The act that caused the harm does not have to have been an intentional act (this is discussed further in chapter 5 when we consider breaches of the duty of care).

Because it is a civil action, an action for negligence has to be proved on the balance of probabilities, that is that one side is more convincing than the other.

Negligence is the most common action brought under tort law.

Ginger beer and a snail

Now we admit that we do like our analogies, and we will be coming back to our milk float shortly, but that is not what this section is about. We are not going to present an analogy involving snails and ginger beer here but a real legal case involving ginger beer and a snail that has had a profound and lasting effect on the law of negligence.

Our aim in discussing this legal case is to show how the law evolves through common law and thus how we have the modern law of negligence in healthcare.

The case is Donoghue v Stevenson [1932]. The date in [ ] is the date that the case was published in the law reports. The case was heard in the House of Lords in December 1931 and the judgment was given in the House of Lords on 26th May 1932. The actual incident happened on 26th August 1928.

Now very few cases of negligence will be heard in the Supreme Court, the successor of the judicial function of the House of Lords. However, legal cases can be slow to go through the legal system, hence our analogy using a milk float, and whilst four years is excessive two years is not that uncommon.

Although the case had a fundamental effect on negligence the facts and the legal argument proposed are quite simple, which is often not the position in cases that are heard in the Supreme Court.

The facts of the case

The facts of the case are relatively straightforward.
- Mrs Donoghue entered a cafe in Paisley with her friend
- The friend bought Mrs Donoghue a bottle of ginger-beer
- The ginger-beer was manufactured by Stevenson

3. WHAT IS NEGLIGENCE?

- The ginger-beer was presented in an opaque bottle and had a metal cap
- Because of the opaqueness of the bottle, it was not possible to see the contents
- The café proprietor removed the metal cap and poured some of the contents of the bottle into a glass which had some ice cream in it
- Mrs Donoghue drank some of the contents of the glass
- Mrs Donoghue's friend poured some of the remaining contents of the bottle of ginger-beer into Mrs Donoghue's glass when a decomposing snail floated out into the glass

Mrs Donoghue claimed that she suffered shock and severe gastroenteritis as a result of the presence of the decomposing snail in the bottle of ginger-beer.

At this point we need to point out that it was never proved that Mrs Donoghue suffered shock or severe gastroenteritis. We are not saying that she didn't, only highlighting that it was not proved in the case but that the court accepted what she said. This is in stark contrast to current negligence in healthcare cases where any harm alleged by a claimant needs to be proved.

Whilst we are discussing what was not proved, the fact that what floated out of the opaque bottle of ginger-beer was a decomposing snail was never proved either. As we shall soon discover, the development of the tort of negligence was founded on an unproven allegation, albeit one that everyone accepted as being true at the time and one that we are not questioning.

Possible legal actions Mrs Donoghue could pursue

Given that the facts of the case indicate that Mrs Donoghue suffered as a result of consuming the ginger-beer drink that was purchased at the café, you may be wondering why Mrs Donoghue did not just make a claim against the café proprietor.

The reason for this is that Mrs Donoghue did not purchase the ginger-beer at the café, in fact it was purchased by her friend. This means that Mrs Donoghue did not enter into a contract with the café. For a legal contract to be formed there have to be four elements established:

- an offer made by one party
- an acceptance by the other party of that offer
- consideration has to be made
- and there has to be an intention to form a legal relationship

An offer was made by the café proprietor, this was for the ginger-beer to be supplied at a specific price. However, there was no acceptance of this offer by Mrs Donoghue, therefore she did not enter into any legal contract with the café proprietor and thus is unable to sue the café proprietor under contract law.

That said, Mrs Donoghue's friend was also made the same offer by the café proprietor, namely for the ginger-beer to be supplied at a specific price. Mrs Donoghue's friend accepted this offer and consideration was made by both parties, the cafe proprietor and Mrs Donoghue's friend, in relation to the offer and acceptance. Consideration means that each party has a benefit as a result of the contract being formed. The café proprietor made a consideration when they supplied the ginger-beer and Mrs Donoghue's friend made a consideration when she paid for the ginger-beer.

The intention to form a legal relationship essentially means that each party to the contract wants the contract to proceed and they know what they are entering into. In this case this was simply the supply and purchase of a bottle of ginger-beer.

3. WHAT IS NEGLIGENCE?

We can see that here was a contract between the café proprietor and Mrs Donoghue's friend regarding the ginger-beer. However, this contract would not allow Mrs Donoghue to bring an action in contract law against the cafe proprietor as the contract was not hers, and Mrs Donoghue's friend did not directly suffer any harm.

Mrs Donoghue could not make a claim against her friend either as she there is no indication that she entered into a contract with her friend for the purchase of the ginger-beer.

Contract law was therefore not an appropriate vehicle for Mrs Donoghue to make a claim against the café proprietor or her friend, if indeed she would have wanted to make a claim against a friend.

This leaves Mrs Donoghue to consider whether she can make a claim against the café proprietor in tort and seek redress under the specific tort of negligence.

Earlier in this chapter it was stated that negligence had legal principles which originated in the 1800s and that these were concerned with what a reasonable person would or would not do.

If we leave everything else to one side for the moment and just consider negligence in relation to reasonableness, would Mrs Donoghue be likely to be successful in a case for negligence against the café proprietor? One way of assessing Mrs Donoghue's chances of being successful in her case against the café proprietor is to decide what actions the café proprietor took and whether those actions were reasonable.

Returning to the facts of the case and identifying those that relate to the actions of the proprietor we can see that:

- The café proprietor sold Mrs Donoghue's friend a bottle of ginger-beer

- The ginger-beer was presented in an opaque bottle and had a metal cap
- Because of the opaqueness of the bottle, it was not possible to see the contents
- The café proprietor removed the metal cap and poured some of the contents of the bottle into a glass which had some ice cream in it

There doesn't seem to be anything contentious with the actions of the café proprietor so far. It is only when Mrs Donoghue's friend pours more ginger-beer from the bottle that the decomposing snail was discovered to have been in the bottle.

The question seems to rely upon whether it is reasonable to expect the seller of an opaque bottle of ginger-beer to be aware that it contained a decomposing snail, or to inspect its contents, by emptying out the whole of the contents of the bottle before having it over to the customer.

Given that it was not possible to see inside the bottle it would be unreasonable to expect the café proprietor to know what the contents were as no one else would be able to tell. This leaves us with the second option.

Whilst there is nothing to stop the café proprietor from serving the ginger-beer by emptying the whole of the contents of the opaque bottle into a glass, is it necessary for them to do so every time they serve ginger-beer? It did not seem to be an issue for Mrs Donoghue or her friend. The ginger-beer was accepted as served, that is some in a glass with ice cream and the rest for Mrs Donoghue or her friend to pour if and when they wanted to.

Although she did not pursue an action against the café proprietor and so it is not possible to determine what would have happened if she had done so, the likely reason that Mrs Donoghue did not take action against the café proprietor is because the actions

3. WHAT IS NEGLIGENCE?

of the café proprietor were seen as being reasonable in the circumstances. It would not have been possible for them to know what was actually in that particular bottle of ginger-beer.

The café proprietor could have sued the manufacturer of the ginger-beer for a breach of contract in supplying a bottle of ginger-beer that was not fit for consumption. However, this would not have helped Mrs Donoghue directly.

Mrs Donoghue's legal action

The legal action that Mrs Donoghue actually pursued was unique at the time and a departure from the accepted legal approach.

Mrs Donoghue decided to sue the manufacturer of the ginger-beer, Stevenson, in negligence. She argued that the manufacturer of the ginger-beer owed her a duty as she was the ultimate consumer.

This was part of the reason that her case was eventually heard in the House of Lords. If Mrs Donoghue was correct an important legal principle would be established which would open up the option of negligence as a course of action far beyond what was currently available at the time.

Lord Atkin who was one of the Law Lords who heard the case in the House of Lords stated that the legal issue before the court was '*whether the manufacturer of an article of drink sold by him to a distributor in circumstances which prevent the distributor or ultimate purchaser or consumer from discovering by inspection any defect is liable under any legal duty to the ultimate purchaser or consumer to take reasonable care that the article is free from defect likely to cause injury to health*' (Donoghue v Stevenson [1932] at page 10).

Stevenson as the manufacturer of the ginger-beer argued through their legal representatives that no such duty existed, and that contract law was the appropriate legal action. It was further argued that to allow Mrs Donoghue's action to proceed would mean that the option of negligence would '*extend to every person who, in lawful circumstances, uses the article made*' (Donoghue v Stevenson [1932] at page 10).

Five Law Lords heard the case in the House of Lords, and it was not a unanimous decision. Three Law Lords gave judgment in favour of Mrs Donoghue and two in favour of Stevenson. Thus, the change in how an action for negligence could be brought, a fundamental change in the legal principles of negligence, was a majority decision.

The legal principle established in Donoghue v Stevenson [1932]

Although Mrs Donoghue ultimately won her case against the manufacturer, Stevenson, of the ginger-beer that caused her to suffer an illness, what is more important is the legal principle that was established through Mrs Donoghue's action for negligence.

As a brief recap of the situation before the judgment in Donoghue v Stevenson [1932], an individual could sue someone if they had a contract with them or if one party had a duty to the other. However, prior to the Donoghue v Stevenson [1932] case, the imposition of a duty on one person to another was legally limited and more closely defined. This meant that the ability of one person to sue another was equally limited.

This changed with the judgment in the Donoghue v Stevenson [1932] case because one of the outcomes of the case was that the legal definition of who had a duty to someone else was vastly expanded. The expansion to whom one person owes a duty to means that the potential number of individuals who could sue that person in negligence was also vastly expanded.

3. WHAT IS NEGLIGENCE?

Lord Atkin stated that the duty is that '*you must take reasonable care to avoid acts or omissions which you can reasonably foresee would be likely to injure your neighbour. Who then, in law, is my neighbour? The answer seems to be persons who are so clearly and directly affected by my act that I ought reasonably to have them in contemplation as being so affected when I am directing my mind to the acts or omissions which are called in question*' (Donoghue v Stevenson [1932] at page 11).

This has become known as the 'neighbour principle'. It is a duty that exists independently of any contract between individuals and means a duty is imposed by law on someone to take reasonable care that their actions, whether an act or omission, does not affect another person who could reasonably be seen to be affected by those actions.

The 'neighbour principle' has resulted in a duty to take reasonable care and this duty of care is explored further in relation to healthcare practice in chapter 4.

Summary of the Donoghue v Stevenson [1932] case

By bringing her action for negligence Mrs Donoghue changed negligence. The judgment in Donoghue v Stevenson [1932] established the 'neighbour principle;' and thus the duty of care we know today, and in doing so opened up negligence in terms of who is able to bring an action for negligence, who can face an action for negligence and what can constitute an action. That is who can sue, who they can sue and what they can sue for were all expanded.

Having established how negligence evolved into the modern law of negligence, the next section considers negligence in healthcare and asks what the difference is between general negligence and negligence in healthcare.

The tort of negligence in healthcare

A major difference between negligence in healthcare compared to other forms of negligence is concerned with where, how and by whom the negligence occurs. The definition of negligence in healthcare that we are using is: negligence that occurs during the care and treatment of a patient or when a patient should be receiving care and/or treatment but doesn't, resulting in harm to the patient.

In the discussion on types of tort it was noted that both negligence and personal injury are torts, that is distinctive and separate torts. Whilst negligence, especially negligence in healthcare, can include an element of personal injury, that is an injury to someone's body, by definition personal injury does not include negligence. This is because in actions for personal injury there is no negligent act that caused the personal injury, if there were a negligent act the action would be for negligence and not personal injury.

Negligence in healthcare is also known as clinical negligence as it relates to the clinical practice of healthcare practitioners. However, we have not used that term as it limits negligence to only being capable of being committed by clinical practitioners acting in the course of their practice. Whereas we believe that negligence in healthcare encompasses all acts and omissions that occur during the care and treatment of a patient, or the care and treatment that should occur, regardless of the setting and that it includes non-clinical members of staff as well.

We recognise that the majority of negligent acts and omissions will be undertake by clinical healthcare practitioners but wanted to have the widest scope in our definition.

3. WHAT IS NEGLIGENCE?

The purpose of negligence in healthcare

We have noted earlier in this chapter that the purpose of tort law is to put someone in the position they would have been had the tort not occurred. As negligence comes under the tort area of law, it is axiomatic that the purpose of negligence is to remedy harm that has been suffered by the claimant by putting them in the position they would have been in had the negligence not occurred.

As negligence in healthcare follows the legal principles and rules of tort law, in particular the tort of negligence, it is equally axiomatic to state that the purpose of negligence in healthcare is to right a wrong that has occurred to the claimant during healthcare by putting them in the position that they would have been in had the negligence not occurred.

That said, it is not as easy to put a person who has suffered negligence in healthcare back in the position they would have been in were it not for the negligent act, as it is with other forms of negligence. For instance, if our beloved milk float had its engine damaged during a routine service because a technician put the wrong part in the engine this could be easily remedied. At worst the technician or the garage could replace the engine completely and compensate the milkman for any loss they suffered such as having to hire a replacement milk float whilst the engine was being replaced.

However, to use a rather simplistic example, if a patient has the wrong eye removed because a surgeon had an x-ray the wrong way round and a healthy functioning eye was removed instead of a diseased one, it would not be possible to put a new eye in to remedy that error.

That said there can be said to be several areas in which negligence in healthcare has a purpose.

The first is that of negligence in general, although it is not possible to always remedy a negligent healthcare act. In relation to negligence in healthcare the purpose is to compensate someone for the harm they have suffered as a result of the negligence that occurred during their care and treatment.

If a claimant, usually the patient who is bringing the claim of negligence in healthcare, succeeds in their case of negligence in healthcare they will be awarded damages. Damages are a sum of money which are designed to put the patient in the position they would have been in had the negligence not occurred, or, and this may be more relevant for negligence in healthcare actions, to ameliorate any issues that have arisen as a consequence of the negligence, such as needing a house that is specially adapted for a disability that now exists that did not before. Damages will also include a sum of money to compensate the individual for such things as the pain and suffering they have endured, loss of earnings and loss of future earnings and possibly a reduced life expectancy (damages are discussed further in chapter 9).

It is important to note that any award made to the claimant is not made to punish the individual who was negligent. The issue of compensation, that is the monetary award or damages as it is more formally known, is discussed further in chapter 9.

That said, although the damages awarded to the claimant are not done so as a punishment against the healthcare practitioner, negligence in healthcare can be seen as a way of holding healthcare practitioners to account for their actions.

Holding a healthcare practitioner accountable means that they are required to give an account, or explanation, of their actions. Healthcare practitioners are accountable for their actions in several ways. These include being accountable to their employer, their healthcare regulatory body, and to the courts. The

3. WHAT IS NEGLIGENCE?

accountability of healthcare practitioners is discussed further in chapter 4 when liability is examined.

In this way negligence in healthcare can be said to be a form of motivation for healthcare practitioners to ensure that their practice is at the appropriate standard and level of competence. For those who do not reach or maintain this standard, negligence in healthcare can result in their removal from the relevant register.

As we will discuss in chapter 10 when examining the effects of negligence, healthcare practitioners are aware of the consequences that an act of negligence could have for them and thus the need to ensure that their practice meets the required standard and what the limit of their competence is and not practise beyond this.

From the above discussion it can be seen that the purpose of negligence in healthcare is to

- where possible revert the patient to the position they would have been in had the negligence not occurred
- provide damages to the patient for any harm or loss they have suffered as a result of not being able to revert back to their original position prior to the negligence occurring, in an effort to ameliorate that harm or loss
- award sufficient damages to the patient, to adequately compensate them in a recognition of the pain or suffering that they have endured
- allow investigation of negligent acts and omissions
- provide a route of accountability for healthcare practitioners
- act as an incentive to healthcare practitioners to ensure that their practice is of a sufficient standard

At its simplest, the purpose of negligence in healthcare is to act as a mechanism for ensuring that a healthcare practitioner who commits a wrong on a patient, either through an act or an omission, is liable for the outcome of their practice. From the patient or claimant perspective it is a mechanism to allow them to seek a remedy for the harm that they have suffered. Whilst for the healthcare practitioner it allows them to establish whether their practice was at the appropriate standard and thus their liability.

The reason that a patient would need to make a claim of negligence in healthcare against a healthcare practitioner (or as it is commonly said, sue a healthcare practitioner) is because patients who receive care and treatment through the NHS do not have a contract with the NHS or Individual healthcare practitioners, and so are unable to sue using contract law.

If a patient were being provided with treatment privately outside of the NHS they would have a contract with their healthcare practitioner providing that treatment and could use contract law to redress any harm that occurred, although they could also use negligence in healthcare as well.

The elements (or wheels) of negligence in healthcare

In order for a patient to bring a successful action for negligence in healthcare they need to be able to prove their case in a civil court on the balance of probabilities. There are four elements that the patient bringing a case alleging negligence in healthcare needs to prove, and identifying these four elements is the function of this section.

One point we would like to make clear is that poor or bad practice by a healthcare practitioner does not mean that the healthcare practitioner has been negligent. Similarly, in an action for negligence in healthcare it is not enough that a

3. WHAT IS NEGLIGENCE?

healthcare practitioner has performed below the standard that a patient expects, or that a mistake has occurred. The tort of negligence requires that for negligence to have been established four specific elements need to be proved, and this applies to negligence in healthcare.

The four elements that have to be proved by a claimant in any case for negligence are:

- The defendant(s) owed them a duty of care
- That this duty of care was breached
- That the claimant suffered harm
- And that the harm was caused by the defendant(s) breach of their duty

If any one of these elements is missing or cannot be proved then the action for negligence will fail. If we return to our analogy of the milk float, each of the elements above is one of the wheels of the milk float. They are what drive a claim of negligence forward. If one of the wheels comes off the milk float or is missing the milk float cannot move forward.

Applying these four elements to negligence in healthcare, we have a patient who becomes the claimant bringing an action for negligence in healthcare against a healthcare practitioner(s) who is (are) the defendant(s).

The patient has to prove that the healthcare practitioner owed them a duty of care, that the healthcare practitioner's practice breached this duty of care by being below the required standard, that they, the patient, suffered harm and that this harm was caused by the defendant's substandard practice.

As with all cases of negligence, if any one of those elements is missing the patient would lose their case for negligence in healthcare. For instance, the healthcare practitioner may be poor at their job or practise below the required standard but if the patient did not suffer harm they would not succeed in an action for negligence in healthcare.

Likewise, if the patient suffered harm but this could not be attributed to the practice of the healthcare practitioner then would also lose their case for negligence in healthcare.

It is only when all four elements of negligence in healthcare are proved that a patient can win their case. Although 'win' is probably not the right word as the harm has still occurred.

If a patient is successful in their claim for negligence in healthcare against a healthcare practitioner, there is no blame attached to the healthcare practitioner as a wrongdoer. This is because in legal use the word negligence is a neutral term, it does not have moral or negative overtones. Rather it is a process for determining if the actions of an individual have reached the required standard. Thus, the action for negligence in healthcare is about the patient claiming and receiving damages for the harm that has occurred to them.

Summary of chapter 3

The rationale behind chapter 3 has been to present an overview of negligence in healthcare by defining what it is and locating it within the legal landscape. This has resulted in a discussion of negligence as a legal principle, and of the types of law that exist.

Negligence has been identified as a specific tort, noting that tort is an aspect of civil law that is concerned with redressing wrongs that have occurred to individuals, attempting where possible to put individuals in the position they would have been in had the wrong not occurred. Further noting that the result of a successful action in tort can result in individuals receiving an award of damages for the wrong that has happened to them.

3. WHAT IS NEGLIGENCE?

Negligence in healthcare has been defined as negligence which occurs during the care and treatment of a patient, specifically that it encompasses all the acts and omissions that occur during the care and treatment of a patient, or the care and treatment that should occur to meet the patient's healthcare need(s).

This led to a discussion of the purpose of negligence in healthcare, which was stated as being to put patients in the position that they would have been in had the negligence not occurred, as is the same with all forms of negligence. However, it was acknowledged that this is less likely to be achieved in negligence in healthcare than other forms of negligence, and it was therefore necessary to provide more appropriate forms of redress for negligence in healthcare through the award of damages. It was identified that although this is a key purpose of negligence in healthcare, the purpose of negligence in healthcare is more than redressing the harm that a patient has suffered and awarding damages, as it is also a mechanism of holding individual healthcare practitioners to account.

Having reviewed and discussed negligence in healthcare as a legal principle and noted its purposes allowed us to identify the four elements that need to be proved for an action in negligence in healthcare to be successful.

The four chapters that follow this chapter each focus on one of the elements of negligence in healthcare and explore it in detail. If we return to our milk float analogy, chapters 4 to 7 are the four wheels of the milk float. They are what drive the case of negligence in healthcare forward:

- chapter 4 examines the duty of care that a healthcare practitioner owes to their patients
- chapter 5 discusses the standard of care and how a breach of the standard is established

- chapter 6 considers what constitutes harm
- chapter 7 is concerned with causation and when harm can be said to have occurred as a result of the breach of the standard of care

CHAPTER 4

DUTY OF CARE

In this chapter we examine the duty of care element of negligence in healthcare. As part of this examination, we consider what a duty of care is and why establishing a duty of care is important in making a claim for negligence in healthcare. This leads us into a discussion on when a duty of care exists in relation to healthcare and who the duty of care is owed to. Following this discussion, we examine liability and what this means and the types of liability that can exist, along with considering specific issues that arise in the liability of healthcare practitioners. Finally, we look at the duty of care in relation to Good Samaritan acts by healthcare practitioners.

Specifically, chapter 4 will answer the question of when a duty of care exists between a healthcare practitioner and a patient.

What is a duty of care?

Back to Marc and his definitions again. A duty is defined as '*an act that is due by legal or moral obligation*' (Curzon 1994). It is an obligation on a person to do something. From our perspective discussing negligence in healthcare, a duty is a legal obligation that a healthcare practitioner has to their patients.

The duty of care is an obligation placed on someone to take reasonable care in their interactions with certain other individuals according to a particular set standard. This means that a healthcare practitioner acting under a duty of care has to meet a particular standard of care. That standard of care is discussed in chapter 5.

Why is it important to consider when a duty of care exists?

Establishing that a duty of care existed in a particular interaction between individuals is vital in claims for negligence. If we consider our milk float for a moment, it was noted that a duty of care is one of the wheels of the milk float driving the milk float forward.

In order for a patient to be successful in their claim of negligence in healthcare against a healthcare practitioner, the patient has to establish that that particular health practitioner owed them a duty of care at the particular time that the patient is claiming the negligence occurred.

The reason that a duty of care has to be established in any claim for negligence, including negligence in healthcare, is that if there is no duty of care there can be no breach of the duty of care and therefore if there is no breach of duty of care no negligence can have occurred. Regardless of what did or did not occur and what someone did or did not do, unless they were acting under a duty of care they cannot be held to account under the tort of negligence.

This is why the duty of care is seen as the first of the four wheels on the milk float. If this particular wheel is missing the milk float cannot be driven correctly and so the negligence case cannot be moved forward. In the same way, if a claimant cannot establish that the defendant owed them a duty of care then they cannot pursue an action in the tort of negligence. There may be other actions available to a person who has suffered harm, but it won't be an action for negligence.

4. DUTY OF CARE

When does a duty of care exist?

Having now recognised that the first question that needs to be answered in a case claiming negligence is whether the claimant is owed a duty of care by the defendant, we can move on to look at when a duty of care exists.

In a claim for negligence in healthcare, if the defendant, the healthcare practitioner, did owe a duty of care to the claimant, the patient, at the relevant time, the case can proceed. The case can also proceed where the issue of whether a duty of care is owed is not decided, that it is still open to debate or argument. It is only where it has been decided that there is no duty of care does the case stall on this issue. This leads us to consider when a duty of care exists.

The neighbour principle revisited

In chapter 3 it was stated that the 'neighbour principle' from the Donoghue v Stevenson [1932] case was used as a way of establishing if one person owes a duty of care to another person.

The duty of care (the neighbour principle) was stated by Lord Atkin in the case as being '*you must take reasonable care to avoid acts or omissions which you can reasonably foresee would be likely to injure your neighbour. Who then, in law, is my neighbour? The answer seems to be persons who are so clearly and directly affected by my act that I ought reasonably to have them in contemplation as being so affected when I am directing my mind to the acts or omissions which are called in question*' (Donoghue v Stevenson [1932] at page 11).

Thus, the precedent that was set in the Donoghue v Stevenson [1932] case is that a person owes a duty of care to another person if that second person could reasonably be said to be affected by the actions of the first person. Either the person undertaking the action will consider that the second person will be affected by their actions, or the first person should consider that the second person will be affected by their actions as any reasonable person would do so. In either way a duty of care is owed.

A development in establishing the duty of care

The Donoghue v Stevenson [1932] case was heard in 1931 and the judgment delivered in 1932. Although it became precedent for issues relating to the duty of care in subsequent actions for negligence and thus had a major effect on the tort of negligence, as was stated in chapter 2, law moves forward. In part this is through common law and changes in legal precedent as new cases emerge with novel legal issues that need to be decided.

A number of negligence related cases have come before the courts that have challenged the 'neighbour principle' as the legal way of establishing if a particular person had a duty of care to a specified other person. Some of these cases have argued that the way of defining the duty of care using the 'neighbour principle' has resulted in situations where a person has been judged to have a duty of care that they could not reasonably have foreseen. That is, that the 'neighbour principle' has been applied too leniently in favour to the person who alleges that they have suffered harm.

A major development relating to duty of care in negligence cases occurred in 1990. The case of Caparo Industries plc v Dickman and others [1990] concerned a company (Caparo) who wished to take over another company and a firm of chartered accountants (Dickman). Caparo bought shares in the other company using information in a set of accounts partly prepared by Dickman as auditors. After taking control of the other company Caparo found that the company it had acquired was not as financially stable as the accounts suggested. Caparo then sued Dickman

4. DUTY OF CARE

in negligence to recover its financial losses in the difference between what the accounts valued the company as and what it was really worth.

The legal issue was whether Dickman owed Caparo a duty of care, and the case was ultimately heard in the House of Lords as the legal principle involved was held to be of sufficient importance due to its significance for future negligence cases.

Strictly applying the precedent from Donoghue v Stevenson [1932] would suggest that Dickman did indeed owe Caparo a duty of care. The accounts were prepared for shareholders, of which Caparo was one. However, Caparo did not use the accounts just as a shareholder but also as an investor. Therefore, it was acknowledged that although a duty of care can be imposed, it is not just the existence of the duty but the scope of the duty of care that is important.

Lord Bridge stated that *'It is never sufficient to ask simply whether A owes B a duty of care. It is always necessary to determine the scope of the duty by reference to the kind of damage from which A must take care to save B harmless.*

"The question is always whether the defendant was under a duty to avoid or prevent that damage, but the actual nature of the damage suffered is relevant to the existence and extent of any duty to avoid or prevent it:" [quoted by Lord Bridge from Brennan J in Sutherland Shire Council v Heyman (1985) 60 ALR. 1 at page 48]

Assuming for the purpose of the argument that the relationship between the auditor of a company and individual shareholders is of sufficient proximity to give rise to a duty of care, I do not understand how the scope of that duty can possibly extend beyond the protection of any individual shareholder from losses in the value of the shares which he holds. As a purchaser of additional shares in reliance on the auditor's report, he stands in no different position from any other investing member of the public to whom the auditor owes no duty' (Caparo Industries plc v Dickman and others [1990] at page 581).

As a result of the recognition that a duty of care comprises not just the existence of the duty but the scope of that duty, the judgment in the Caparo Industries plc v Dickman and others [1990] was that Dickman did owe a duty of care to Caparo but only as a shareholder and not as an investor. This was because to impose a duty upon Dickman to all potential investors would be too onerous upon them. Caparo thus lost their case for negligence against Dickman.

As well as deciding the outcome in the actual case, the judgment in Caparo Industries plc v Dickman and others [1990] established a new 3 stage test for determining the existence of a duty of care in negligence cases.

The Caparo 3 stage test

Following Caparo Industries plc v Dickman and others [1990], the three stages that a court would consider before deciding that a duty of care exists between two parties are:

- reasonable foreseeability
- proximity
- justice and reasonableness

This results in three questions that a court has to have answered:

- was the harm that occurred reasonably foreseeable?
- what is the proximity of the relationship between the two parties?
- is it just and reasonable that a duty of care is imposed on the defendant?

4. DUTY OF CARE

The questions relating to reasonable foreseeability and proximity are closely related to the 'neighbour principle' from the Donoghue v Stevenson [1932] case. The question relating to justice and reasonableness is a new element in establishing the existence of a duty of care.

As an illustration of how the 3-stage test from Caparo Industries plc v Dickman and others [1990] works, if Andy were to sue Marc in negligence, Andy would be the claimant and Marc the defendant. The questions for the court hearing the case of Nichols v Cornock would be:

- did Marc reasonably foresee that Andy could be harmed by his actions, or should Marc have reasonably foreseen that Andy could be harmed by his actions?
- what is the proximity of the relationship between Marc and Andy?
- is it just and reasonable that a duty be placed on Marc to take care specifically in relation to Andy?

The answers to these three questions will result in the decision of whether Marc owed Andy a duty of care.

If we unpack these three questions, we can see that the first, relating to reasonably foreseeing that someone could be harmed by Marc's actions, is essentially just another way of stating the 'neighbour principle' from the Donoghue v Stevenson [1932] case. Another way of stating the question is to ask if Marc can reasonably be expected to foresee that if he did not take care in his actions Andy would be harmed by those actions. If Andy is foreseeable as someone who could be potentially harmed by Marc's actions there is a duty to him.

The second question relating to proximity is asking the same as when the test from Donoghue v Stevenson [1932] asks who is my neighbour? Another way of asking about proximity is to ask if there is a legal relationship between Marc and Andy, not as in a familial or personal relationship but are Marc and Andy sufficiently close to each other that one's actions could affect the other. Proximity means that something close to each other is related but if they are far apart they are unrelated and not proximate.

One way of looking at proximity is to ask if Marc would know, or should know, that Andy was of a type of person who would be affected by his actions. As an example of proximity or a legal relationship, we can consider the proximity that exists between a driver and a pedestrian on a road. If a driver drives to a standard that is below what is acceptable, a pedestrian who they harm who is sufficiently close that the driver would have a duty of care to them. This is because the pedestrian is seen as a 'neighbour' of the driver in relation to the driver being capable of causing harm to the pedestrian through not taking sufficient care and attention in their driving. The pedestrian is a type of person who would be affected by the actions of a driver.

In the proximity test the claimant has to prove that the duty was owed to them, that is a specific type of person, and that the defendant should have them, or that specific type of person, in mind when reasonably foreseeing if someone could be harmed by their actions.

An example of the lack of proximity in a legal case examining a medical issue

Examining when proximity was said not to exist in a legal case involving a medical issue can assist us in determining what proximity is.

In Goodwill v British Pregnancy Advisory Service [1996], Mrs Goodwill brought an action for negligence against the British Pregnancy Advisory Service on the grounds that her lover, Mr

4. DUTY OF CARE

MacKinlay, had had a vasectomy, performed by the defendants, some three years earlier before she knew him. Mr MacKinlay had been told, after two semen samples were tested, that the vasectomy as a success.

Because of the vasectomy the couple did not use contraception and Mrs Goodwill became pregnant and sued for the expense involved with the childbirth and bringing up the child, including loss of employment income.

It was acknowledged that a doctor owed MacKinlay a duty of care. The question was whether the defendants owed a duty of care to Mrs Goodwill.

It was held that there was no proximity between the defendants and Mrs Goodwill. This is because the defendants could not have contemplated Mrs Goodwill at the time of the procedure. As Lord Justice Gibson said *'how the defendants knew or should have known that their advice [regarding the success of the vasectomy] would be communicated to ...[Mrs Goodwill] and relied upon by her as ... a warranty or permanent infertility when she did not meet, or commence a sexual relationship with Mr MacKinlay until three years later, it is not apparent'* (Goodwill v British Pregnancy Advisory Service [1996] at page 168).

It was suggested by Lord Justice Gibson in the case that had Mrs Goodwill been Mr MacKinlay's wife or partner and the doctor performing the vasectomy was aware that the procedure was for her benefit as well as his, it is likely that the defendants would have had a duty of care to her. However, at the time of the procedure *'they had no knowledge of her, she was not an existing sexual partner of Mr MacKinlay but was merely, like any other woman in the world, a potential future sexual partner of his, that is to say a member of an indeterminately large number of females who might have sexual relations with*

Mr MacKinlay during his lifetime' (Goodwill v British Pregnancy Advisory Service [1996] at page 169). And as such, there was no proximity between the defendants and Mrs Goodwill.

As there was no proximity there could be no duty of care and as a result Mrs Goodwill lost her case for negligence.

This case demonstrates that just because there is a relationship between a healthcare practitioner and their patients which results in a duty of care existing, this duty does not extend to everyone who could be said to have an interest in the outcome of a healthcare procedure. It has to have been reasonable for the healthcare practitioner to have contemplated them at the time the procedure was performed, otherwise proximity will not be said to exist.

Proximity and public policy

Usually, if it is reasonably foreseeable that harm could occur to the claimant then the issue of proximity is satisfied and the first two stages of the duty of care test can be satisfied at the same time.

The third part of the Caparo Industries plc v Dickman and others [1990] three stage test relating to whether it is just and reasonable to impose a duty of care is a public policy matter. This aspect of the three-stage test only arises if the first two stages have indicated that a duty of care exists between the defendant and the claimant.

By asking if it is just and reasonable that a duty of care is placed upon the defendant allows the court to consider what the result of imposing the duty may do in future cases. For instance, imposing a duty in a specific case may mean that the door is opened for many other individuals in a similar situation to the claimant to pursue an action for negligence, when this is not in the public interest. This third stage of the test from Caparo Industries plc v Dickman and others [1990] effectively asks if imposing a duty of care on the defendant is in the public benefit or not. If it isn't then the duty of care will not exist. As an example, imposing a duty on police officers or the police service in relation to certain aspects of their role such as successfully investigating a specific crime has not been seen to be in the public benefit. Three related reasons can be advanced for this position, the first is that it may hamper the police in their role as they are more concerned with not being sued for negligence than performing their role, the second is that more individuals would use the police at a cost to the public, whilst the third is that if the police owe a duty of care then what other public servants would also have to have a duty of care imposed upon them and where would this end.

Special relationships

A duty of care is more likely to be established if the claimant is at a disadvantage to the defendant. This is especially so if the defendant is in a position of 'power' to the claimant. These are generally known as special relationships.

Such relationships include:

- family relationships such as parent and child
- teacher and pupil
- when the complaint is in some way dependent upon the defendant
- where the claimant relies upon a special skill that the defendant has

The relationship between a healthcare practitioner and their patient is a form of special relationship. The patient is dependent upon the knowledge and skills of the healthcare practitioner and this places the healthcare practitioner in a position of power in relation to the patient.

It fact, it is a recognised and established matter of law that in healthcare all healthcare practitioners have a duty of care to their patients, where the healthcare practitioner is undertaking their normal and recognised duties and practice. This also includes student healthcare practitioners.

Indeed, very often in cases of negligence in healthcare the issue of whether a duty of care was owed by the healthcare practitioner to the patient is not even contested but agreed at the outset of the case. The question that is asked in relation to the duty of care is not whether the duty exists but what the scope of a healthcare practitioner's duty is to this particular patient. This is something we will come back to in the chapters that follow.

Who is the duty of care owed to?

Having established what a duty of care means and when it can be said to exist, it is appropriate to now consider who a healthcare practitioner owes a duty of care to. Answering this question is the focus of this section.

According to the 'neighbour principle' from the Donoghue v Stevenson [1932] case the duty of care is to those who can reasonably be said to be affected by your actions. Also remembering that the Caparo Industries plc v Dickman and others [1990] case amended this by introducing a requirement that there be proximity between the two individuals before a duty of care is owed by one to the other.

Additionally, when discussing special relationships above it was stated that the relationship between a healthcare practitioner and their patient is a relationship that is seen as a special

4. DUTY OF CARE

relationship and thus one where a duty of care is said to exist without the need to prove that it exists.

The issue that needs to be addressed to answer the question of who a healthcare practitioner owed a duty of care to therefore appears to rest on when is a patient a patient, that is at what point the duty arises.

It may be obvious to say but if a person is an existing patient of a healthcare practitioner then that healthcare practitioner has a duty of care to that patient. It is possible to rephrase this as if a patient is before a healthcare practitioner they have a duty of care to them.

However, when does someone who the healthcare practitioner has never met and has not cared for or treated previously become a patient of that healthcare practitioner? There has to be a point at which that person becomes a patient of the healthcare practitioner. Otherwise because of the special skills that a healthcare practitioner has they could be said to have a special relationship with everyone who has need of those special skills. This would potentially impose a duty of care on the healthcare practitioner for everyone.

Given that healthcare practitioners work within different professions, such as nurse or paramedic or physiotherapist, and even within those professions they specialise, so that there are community nurses and intensive care nurses and infectious disease nurses and oncology nurses, not all healthcare practitioners are the same and the special skills they have are different. Meaning that not all healthcare practitioners will have the appropriate skills and knowledge and competencies that the patient requires to address their healthcare needs.

Just because a patient is before a particular healthcare practitioner does not mean that that healthcare practitioner is the one who is best placed to assist the patient in meeting their healthcare need.

The legal answer to the question of when is a patient a patient, and so when does a healthcare practitioner have a duty of care for a particular person, is that a relationship between a healthcare practitioner and a patient is said to exist when the healthcare practitioner assumes responsibility for the patient, or for some aspect of their care and treatment.

For general practitioners, the assumption of responsibility occurs when the patient is accepted onto the general practitioner's or the healthcare practice's list of patients.

If we were to consider a patient who arrived at an accident and emergency department and was subsequently admitted to a medical ward, different healthcare practitioners would owe the patient a duty of care at different times depending upon when they assumed responsibility for an aspect of the patient's care. Thus, the healthcare practitioners working in the accident and emergency department would have a duty of care to the patient prior to those healthcare practitioners working on the medical ward.

However, the case of Barnett v Chelsea & Kensington Hospital Management Committee [1968] is a useful illustration of the special relationship that exists in healthcare and the duty of care owed by healthcare providers and healthcare practitioners.

The incident in this case occurred on the 1st of January 1966. Three nightwatchmen had drunk some tea and started vomiting shortly afterwards. At 8am, a few hours later, all three walked to the casualty department (as Accident and Emergency Departments were then called) of the hospital. The casualty department was open, and the men were able to speak to a nurse (Nurse Corbett) stating that all three of them had

4. DUTY OF CARE

started persistently vomiting after drinking some tea. The nurse telephoned the doctor (Dr Banerjee) who was the casualty officer at the time and informed him of the men's situation, it is stated that the casualty officer was unwell himself and instead of going to see the men he told the nurse to inform them to see their GPs.

Barnett was one of the three night watchmen, and he died a few hours later from arsenic poisoning. His estate sued the hospital for negligence in respect of the casualty officer not seeing and treating him.

One of the issues which had to be decided in the case was whether the hospital, the casualty officer, and/or the nurse owed a duty of care to Mr Barnett. Although it has just been stated that a healthcare practitioner owes a patient a duty of care when they assume responsibility for a patient and use their professional knowledge and skills in caring and treating the patient. As we will shortly see, this is not the case in an Accident and Emergency department, as the duty on them is more onerous.

In his judgment Justice Nield stated that he had '*to determine the duty of those who provide and run a casualty department when a person presents himself at that department complaining of illness or injury and before he is treated and received into the hospital wards. This is not a case of a casualty department which closes its doors and said that no patients can be received. The three Watchmen entered the defendants' hospital without hindrance, they made complaints to the nurse who received them and she in turn passed those complaints onto the medical casualty officer, and he sent a message through the nurse reporting to advise the three men. Is there, on these facts, shown to be created a relationship between the three watchmen and the hospital staff such as gives rise to a duty of care in the defendants which they owe to the three men?*'

Justice Nield answered his question by noting '*in my judgment, there was here such a close and direct relationship between the hospital and the watchmen that there was imposed on the hospital a duty of care which they owed to the watchmen. Thus I have no doubt that nurse Corbett and doctor Banerjee were under a duty to the deceased*' (Barnett v Chelsea & Kensington Hospital Management Committee [1968] at page 1072).

We will return to the case of Barnett v Chelsea & Kensington Hospital Management Committee [1968] when we consider causation in chapter 7.

What is important about the judgment in this case is that it established that the healthcare practitioners who work in accident and emergency departments owe a duty of care to the individuals who turn up with a healthcare complaint. That is unless, as Justice Nield notes, the accident and emergency department is closed to new patients. The hospital providing the services of the accident and emergency department also owe a duty of care to those who enter the department.

The duty of care owed by healthcare practitioners in an accident and emergency department is thus not based on an assumed responsibility for the patient but on the fact that the patient is within the department.

There are therefore two aspects to the special relationship between a healthcare practitioner and patients, whether the healthcare practitioner has assumed a responsibility for the patient, or if the patient has requested assistance within an accident and emergency department where the healthcare practitioner is currently working.

An important point to make about to whom a duty of care is owed to is that the duty is to take care, not to provide care. This is something that we will discuss further in chapter 5 when examining what the standard of care is.

4. DUTY OF CARE

An aside; a person to whom you do not owe a duty of care and to whom you do not have a prior relationship is normally referred to as a stranger in legal discussion, as it is in normal everyday speech.

Liability

In chapter 3 when discussing the purpose of negligence in healthcare, the accountability of healthcare practitioners was raised. Although accountability is easily defined, it is often confused with responsibility and liability. Indeed, the three terms are often used interchangeably when they are in fact distinct concepts.

Returning to Marc's use of definitions. According to the Shorter Oxford English Dictionary responsibility is '*a charge, trust, or duty, for which one is responsible*', accountability is '*liable to be called to account*', whilst liability is '*answerable by law*' (Stevenson 2007). Whereas in a legal dictionary liability is seen as being '*subject to a disadvantage at law*' (Penner 2001).

The relationship between the three concepts, responsibility, accountability and liability, is important because it informs us as to what the outcomes of a healthcare practitioner's duty of care could be.

If a healthcare practitioner was only responsible for the care they provide once they had undertaken that care it would be the end of their involvement. There would be no comeback on them if anything went wrong.

On the other hand, if the healthcare practitioner was accountable for the care they provide, they could be called to account for the care they provided. Whereas if the healthcare practitioner was liable for the care they provide then not only would they have to give an account of their actions, but they would also have to satisfy those to whom they were giving their account or face the liability aspect which would be being disadvantaged at law, that is face a penalty of some kind. Liability is sometimes said to be accountability with the possibility or a penalty or punishment.

Having defined these three terms, we can see that in relation to negligence in healthcare and the healthcare practitioner's duty of care it is the liability of the healthcare practitioner that can result in them facing an action for negligence.

To have a liability for their duty of care means that the healthcare practitioner has to give an account of how they met their duty of care and may face a legal penalty if they have not satisfied those to whom they give their account that they have discharged their duty of care to the necessary standard (the standard for a duty of care is discussed in chapter 5).

In relation to a duty of care in healthcare, the healthcare practitioner's liability is to fulfil their legal obligation to take reasonable care in their actions with their patients, and not to cause them harm through their actions or omissions.

A healthcare practitioner's areas of accountability liability

The rest of this section will consider some of the ways in which a healthcare practitioner is held to account and may face a liability. Just to reiterate, a healthcare practitioner will only face a liability if their account is not deemed to be sufficient.

If a healthcare practitioner is an employee, they will be accountable to their employer for their actions, through their contract of employment. If the account given by the employed healthcare practitioner is not sufficient for the employer the healthcare practitioner may face a disciplinary investigation and possible sanction. The ultimate liability for the employed

4. DUTY OF CARE

healthcare practitioner is the sanction of being dismissed from their position.

Most healthcare practitioners are required by law to be registered with one of the healthcare regulatory bodies. The healthcare regulatory bodies and the healthcare practitioners they regulate are:

- General Chiropractic Council – chiropractors
- General Dental Council – dentists and other dental care practitioners including clinical dental technicians, dental hygienists, dental nurses, dental technicians, dental therapists, and orthodontic therapists
- General Medical Council – doctors
- General Optical Council – dispensing opticians and optometrists
- General Osteopathic Council – osteopaths
- General Pharmaceutical Council or in Northern Ireland, the Pharmaceutical Society of Northern Ireland – pharmacists and pharmacy technicians
- Health and Care Professions Council – arts therapists, biomedical scientists, chiropodists and podiatrists, clinical scientists, dietitians, hearing aid dispensers, occupational therapists, operating department practitioners, orthoptists, paramedics, physiotherapists, practitioner psychologists, prosthetists and orthotists, radiographers, and speech and language therapists
- Nursing and Midwifery Council – midwives, nurses and nursing associates

A function of the healthcare regulatory bodies is to ensure that the public is protected from incompetent healthcare practitioners. To achieve this, they have five key areas of responsibility:

- they maintain a register of individuals who are entitled to practise as a healthcare practitioner for their respective professional areas. For instance, the General Medical Council maintains the register of individuals entitled to practise as a medical doctor, and the Nursing and Midwifery Council maintains the register of those entitled to practise as a nurse or midwife
- they set the standard of initial education for those who want to register with them
- they set the level of competence that a healthcare practitioner has to maintain in order to continue to hold their registration to practise
- they produce codes of conduct, and ethical standards, that their respective healthcare practitioners are expected to adhere to
- they investigate the fitness to practise of those healthcare practitioners on their respective registers

The relevance of negligence in healthcare is that if a healthcare practitioner is found to have committed a negligent act this can result in them also facing a fitness to practise hearing with their healthcare regulatory body which will determine if they are able to practise at the appropriate level of competence. If the healthcare practitioner is found to have impaired fitness to practise they may face the liability of being sanctioned by their healthcare regulatory body.

These sanctions can include: warnings and reprimands; having a condition put on the healthcare practitioner's practice such as being made to retrain in a specific area of their practice, only being allowed to practise under supervision; being temporarily removed from the register, for periods up to 12 months, and thus unable to practise for the specified period of time; or they may face the ultimate sanction of being removed entirely from the register and thus unable to practise.

4. DUTY OF CARE

The final area of accountability that we need to raise is that of the healthcare practitioner's accountability to a court of law. If an action brought by a patient for negligence in healthcare goes to court the healthcare practitioner(s) will be required to give their account of what happened. This may be by a written statement or as oral evidence in the courtroom.

If the court judges that the healthcare practitioner's practice has fallen below the required standards it may make the healthcare practitioner liable by deciding in the patient's favour and sanction the healthcare practitioner by making an award against them.

The healthcare practitioner will also have criminal liability under the criminal law.

Liability issues

Although individual healthcare practitioners have liability for their duty of care to their patients, there are several issues relating to liability which need to be considered to complete our understanding of liability in relation to negligence in healthcare. These issues are concerned with: vicarious lability and when someone else can have liability for a healthcare practitioner's actions, including what acting in the course of employment means; the liability of student healthcare practitioners; what indemnity is and when it might be needed by a healthcare practitioner; team liability; and, how liability is affected by delegation.

Vicarious liability

Vicarious liability has existed since the early to mid-1800s. Initially it was known as the master/servant law and its effect was that a 'servant' undertaking their 'master's' orders were exempt from personal liability for their actions, with the liability falling on the 'master' issuing the instructions because the 'master' could control the actions of the 'servant'.

Eventually the master/servant law expanded to include all those who were employed and became known as vicarious liability. Vicarious liability is still an aspect of employment law and means that although a person who commits a negligent act is liable in law, employers are also liable for the actions of their employees acting in the course of their employment. Under vicarious liability the employer is liable for the acts and omissions of its employees who are acting in the course of their employment, and this includes any acts or omissions which are deemed to be negligent. That is, it is an employer who may have to suffer the legal penalty that arises as a consequence of the employee's actions.

Vicarious liability is also sometimes referred to as institutional liability as it is the institution or organisation that takes on liability for its employees or members. This does not mean that the healthcare practitioner has their liability taken away from them. This is not the case; the healthcare practitioner retains their liability, but the employer is also liable.

In relation to negligence in healthcare the existence of vicarious liability should be welcomed as it means that there is someone who can attempt to remedy the harm that has occurred to the patient, or if necessary pay any award of damages. After all, a healthcare organisation that employs healthcare practitioners is more likely to have the resources to affect a remedy than an individual healthcare practitioner, and to be brutally blunt, a healthcare organisation is going to have more money to pay an award of damages than an individual healthcare practitioner. It can be said that if an employer has the benefit of the healthcare practitioner's services then they should also bear the burden if something untoward happens.

4. DUTY OF CARE

Additionally, an employer who has vicarious liability for the actions of their employees is more likely to insist that employees work within their level of competence and to maintain a high standard of healthcare practice by those employees.

In an action for negligence in healthcare, the claimant would pursue action against the individual healthcare practitioner through their employer to ensure that vicarious liability means that any award they receive is made by the employer.

That vicarious liability exists in a healthcare context was established by the case of Cassidy v Ministry of Health [1951]. In that case a patient who had some bones reset in his wrist suffered stiff fingers as a consequence of negligence by one of the surgeons who operated on him.

The Ministry of Health, which ran the hospital where the patient was treated and employed the surgeon, stated that they could not be held liable as the surgeon was not a servant of theirs as they could not control the way in which the surgeon performed their role.

It was held in the case that if the surgeon was employed and paid by the hospital authorities and not the patient then the hospital authorities were liable for the actions of the surgeon. As Lord Justice Denning stated, *'the reason why the employers are liable in such cases is not because they can control the way in which work is done – they often have not sufficient knowledge to do so – but because they employ the staff and have chosen them for the task and have in their hands the ultimate sanction for good conduct – the power of dismissal'* (Cassidy v Ministry of Health [1951] at page 360).

Vicarious liability therefore applies to those who work under a contract of employment within healthcare settings. However, healthcare practitioners who work as independent contractors are not covered under the law of vicarious liability. Further to this, even if an employee is working under a contract of employment they would only be covered by vicarious liability if they were working in the course of their employment at the time of the event in question.

Proving that they work under a contract of employment should be relatively easy for a healthcare practitioner to do. Proving that they were acting in the course of their employment can be more difficult for the healthcare practitioner.

Acting in the course of employment

It was just noted that although a healthcare practitioner may easily prove that they are an employee working under a contract of employment, for instance by showing their contract of employment, it is more difficult for them to show that they were acting in the course of their employment at the time an incident occurred. This section therefore looks at how the law views whether someone is working within the course of their employment or not.

The following legal cases demonstrate some of the issues in deciding whether someone may be said to lawfully be considered to be acting in the course of their employment or not.

In the case of Limpus v London General Omnibus Co. (1863) the court heard that in 1861 an omnibus driver working for the London General Omnibus Co. pulled his omnibus directly across the path of an omnibus belonging to Limpus on purpose. In so doing he caused considerable damage to Limpus' omnibus and to their horses. Limpus sued the London General Omnibus Co. on the basis that the driver was acting in the course of his employment with them.

The London General Omnibus Co. argued that they were not liable under the master/servant law, as it then was, as they had

4. DUTY OF CARE

expressly informed their drivers and issued them with a card of regulations which stated that they *'must not, on any account, race with, or obstruct, another omnibus, or hinder or annoy any driver or conductor thereof, whether such omnibus be one belonging to the company or otherwise'* (Limpus v London General Omnibus Co. (1863) at page 557).

London General Omnibus Co. were effectively saying that if an employee does something which is outside of their stated regulations that employee cannot be said to be acting in the course of their employment.

However, the case was found against London General Omnibus Co. and they were held to be liable for the action of their driver. Justice Willams stated that *'if a master employs a servant to drive and manage a carriage, the master is, in my opinion, answerable for any misconduct of the servant in driving or managing which can fairly be considered to have resulted from the performance of the functions entrusted to him, and especially if he was acting for this master's benefit, and not for any purpose of furthering his own interest'* (Limpus v London General Omnibus Co. (1863) at page 559).

By acting as he did the driver was doing so to further his employer's interests, even if the manner in which he did so was not one permitted by the employer.

In the case of Storey v Ashton [1869], Ashton was a wine merchant who sent two employees, to make a delivery. On the return journey, which was outside normal business hours, the two employees went to the property of the brother-in-law of one of them which was in the opposite direction to the one they needed to take to return to the wine merchants. During their diversion the two employees ran over Mr Storey, who sued Ashton on the basis that he employed the two men responsible for his injuries.

The legal issue was whether the two employees were acting in the course of their employment during their diversion from their return route. The court held that as the employees were operating outside of normal business hours and were taking a journey that was independent of the journey they needed to take they were not acting in the course of their employment but were instead acting on a frolic of their own and thus Ashton was not liable for their actions.

The case of Century Insurance Co. Ltd v Northern Ireland Road Transport Board [1942] involved a petrol tanker driver who when delivering petrol to a garage started the transfer of petrol from the tanker to the garage's storage tank and as the petrol was transferring lit a cigarette and then threw the lighted match away. As a consequence, an explosion occurred.

Damage was caused to the petrol tanker, a parked motor car, several houses and parts of the garage. Century Insurance Co. Ltd were the insurers of Northern Ireland Road Transport Board who operated the petrol tanker.

The legal issue in the case that concerns us is, was the driver acting in the course of his employment when he smoked the cigarette therefore making the delivery company vicariously liable for his actions?

Viscount Simon Lord chancellor stated that the driver's 'duty was to watch over the delivery of the spirit into the tank, to see that it did not overflow, and to turn off the tap when the proper quantity had passed from the tanker. In circumstances like these, "they also serve who only stand and wait". He was presumably close to the apparatus, and his negligence in starting smoking and in throwing away a lighted match at that moment is plainly negligent in the discharge of his duties upon which he was employed' (Century Insurance Co. Ltd v Northern Ireland Road Transport Board [1942] at page 494).

4. DUTY OF CARE

Thus, although the driver can be said to be stupid and negligent, he was doing what he was employed to do and therefore acting in the course of his employment.

The final case we will consider is that of Iqbal v London Transport Executive [1973]. This is another case involving the driving of a bus. However, in this case Iqbal was a bus conductor who had been expressly told by his employer, London Transport Executive, not to drive buses. Regardless he drove a bus at the bus depot and injured a fellow employee when he hit them with the bus. The fellow employee sued London Transport Executive for the negligent action of Iqbal. London Transport Executive argued that Iqbal was not acting in the course of his employment when he hit and injured his fellow employee.

The court held that Iqbal was employed as a conductor and that was his duty. It was stated that by expressly prohibiting Iqbal from driving a bus his employer had limited the scope of his employment so that it did not include driving a bus. Therefore, at the time Iqbal was driving the bus he could not be acting in the course of his employment, even though it was during his working day, and so London Transport Executive were not vicariously liable for his actions.

From the above case the following can be stated:

- An employer is vicariously liable for the actions of its employees where the employee is acting in the course of their employment, for example according to a job description or the details within a contract of employment
- An employer is vicariously liable for the actions of its employees where the employee is acting in the furtherance of the employer's interests
- An employer is not liable for the actions of its employees where the employee is acting outside of the scope of their employment, for example if they are on a frolic of their

own. A frolic of their own is an act that is not related to their work but rather something done for themselves
- If the employee is undertaking an act for which they are employed but does it in an unauthorised manner or a negligent manner the employer will still have vicarious liability for that act

The liability of students

As mentioned in the section on special relationships, students have a duty of care to their patients and thus have liability in relation to this. However, a student is not an employee of the healthcare organisation, but rather on a clinical placement arranged by their education establishment and so cannot act in the course of their employment.

Whilst this may appear to be an issue at first, it is not because the student has a contract with their education provider which will detail what their role and duties are during a clinical placement. It is this which would be used to determine if a student is acting in the 'course of their employment', or on a frolic of their own.

With regard to the vicarious liability for a student on a clinical placement, the healthcare organisation will provide this, although the education provider may also have vicarious liability for the student's actions as well. When clinical placements are initially agreed there is a legal agreement between the educational provider and healthcare organisation as to who is vicariously liable for harm caused by the students actions and also who is liable for injuries caused to the student.

Indemnity

Healthcare practitioners who are self-employed cannot be covered by vicarious liability as they do not work for an

4. DUTY OF CARE

employer. They are their own employer. Therefore, if something were to go wrong they are liable for both their own actions and also for any financial redress that may be ordered by a court.

Additionally, some healthcare practitioners take on roles outside of their contracted employment for voluntary associations and for other organisations who do not employ them. This is where indemnity cover comes in. Indemnity can be defined as *'security or protection against hurt, damage or loss'* according to the Shorter Oxford English Dictionary (Stevenson 2007). Indemnity cover is a form of insurance policy which is designed to provide assistance in the event that the policyholder faces certain events, such as being sued for negligence in healthcare.

The assistance that can be provided under indemnity cover may include legal assistance with dealing with the claim against them and/or for the payment of a financial award made as a result of losing a negligence case.

All the healthcare regulatory bodies require those healthcare practitioners who are registered with them to have some form of indemnity cover in place. Usually for those healthcare practitioners who are employed the vicarious liability that their employers provide meets this requirement for indemnity cover. However, those healthcare practitioners who are self-employed or take on additional roles outside of their main employment need to have their own indemnity cover arranged.

There are specialist organisations who provide indemnity cover for healthcare practitioners for a fee. Some professional organisations and trade unions provide indemnity cover for their members as part of their member subscription.

Any healthcare practitioner taking out independent indemnity cover for their clinical practice needs to be aware that there are two forms of cover available. One provides protection for any incident which occurs whilst a premium is being paid but once the healthcare practitioner stops paying their cover ends even for past incidents which come to light after the premiums have stopped being paid. The other provides indemnity for any period where a premium was paid, even if the healthcare practitioner later stops paying their premiums.

At its simplest indemnity covers healthcare practitioners against the costs of defending a legal case for negligence in healthcare and any award for damages made in the case. It may also provide legal and ethical advice to a healthcare practitioner if they are uncertain of a specific course of action, for instance if they can obtain consent from a patient under the age of sixteen or whether they have to seek consent from a parent. Some forms of indemnity cover also provide assistance to healthcare practitioners who are facing a criminal case or a fitness to practise hearing by their healthcare regulatory body. The provision of advice by an indemnity provider is designed to assist the healthcare practitioner in meeting their duties to their patients and so reduce the possibility of a complaint or claim for negligence in healthcare against them.

Team liability

Healthcare practitioners generally work as part of a healthcare team to meet the healthcare needs of a patient. It is often thought that if a member of a healthcare team breaches their duty of care then it is the team as a whole that is liable for this. That there is a collective responsibility for the actions taken within the team. This is incorrect.

This was confirmed in the case of Wilsher v Essex Area Health Authority [1986] which had to consider whether individual staff members of a special care baby unit had been negligent by incorrectly assessing a baby's oxygen levels which had resulted in the baby receiving excess oxygen causing the baby to become virtually blind.

The court found for the baby and awarded damages to them via their mother who brought the case on their behalf.

As well as presenting its judgment on the facts of the case, the court also declared that there is no legal concept of team liability. Each and every member of a healthcare team is individually liable for their own actions. The reason why there is no team liability is that in an action for negligence an assessment is made of the actions of individuals and asks whether they have fulfilled their duty of care. Any decision is made on an individual basis. It is possible that several individuals in a team could all be found to be negligent, but each is assessed separately. A healthcare team would not be held to be negligent as a whole, rather an individual member(s) of the team would be judged to be negligent.

As well as noting that there is no concept of team liability in law, it is equally worth pointing out that senior members of a team are not liable for the junior members of a healthcare team simply because they are the senior members or the team leader(s). Each and every member of the healthcare team is personally liable for their own actions, and this includes the junior members of the team.

One aspect of working within a healthcare team that can result in some healthcare practitioners believing that they are under the liability of someone else is in relation to 'orders'. Some healthcare practitioners consider that if they are asked to do something by a more senior member of the healthcare team they are acting under their 'orders'. This is not the case. No-one can order a healthcare practitioner, no matter how junior or inexperienced, to do something that they either do not consider appropriate or do not feel they are competent to do.

The junior healthcare practitioner may feel that they are being pressurised but part of the individual liability each healthcare practitioner has is to work within their competencies and to only do what they consider is in the patient's best interests or what the patient has consented to. If the request, or 'order', falls outside of either, or both, of those two elements then the junior healthcare practitioner should explain why they cannot undertake the task. They could also ask to be shown how to do the task first and/or to be supervised whilst they perform the task to ensure that it is performed correctly.

Delegation and liability

Healthcare practitioners can delegate tasks to other healthcare practitioners, usually those healthcare practitioners junior to themselves. When a healthcare practitioner does delegate a task to another healthcare practitioner they retain liability for ensuring that the task is completed and to the appropriate standard. The healthcare practitioner who the task is delegated to also has liability for the task as well.

In addition, the healthcare practitioner who delegated the task has a liability for ensuring that the task was appropriately delegated, that is to someone who is competent to undertake the task and has the capacity and all the relevant information to undertake it.

In a similar way, a healthcare practitioner who has a task delegated to them has a liability to ensure that they should only accept it if it is within their competence, and they have the capacity to take on the task.

It may be necessary for the healthcare practitioner who delegated a task to provide supervision regarding the performance and completion of the task, although this is not always necessary.

4. DUTY OF CARE

A healthcare practitioner delegating a task to another will fulfil their liability if they delegate appropriately, provide the correct level of supervision, if needed, and give adequate instruction. If they do this and the healthcare practitioner to whom the task was delegated still acts negligently then the liability will rest with that healthcare practitioner and not the one who delegated the task to them.

Good Samaritan acts

A Good Samaritan is someone who voluntarily assists another.

The legal position regarding voluntary acts of assistance was discussed in the F v West Berkshire Health Authority [1989] case. This case was concerned with whether it would be lawful to sterilise a female who was unable to make the decision herself. When giving the judgment in the case, which was that it would be lawful to provide the sterilisation, Lord Goff stated *the 'doctor in the house' who volunteers to assist a lady in the audience who, overcome by the drama or by the heat in the theatre, has fainted away is impelled to act by no greater duty that that imposed by his own Hippocratic Oath'* (F v West Berkshire Health Authority [1989] at page 567).

As a result, it is clear that here is no legal requirement for someone to assist another unless they have a pre-existing duty of care to that person. Although Lord Goff refers to doctors, the legal principle that there is no Good Samaritan law in the United Kingdom applies to all healthcare practitioners.

It has been said earlier in this chapter that it is rare that the duty of care is a matter of dispute in a case of negligence in healthcare that involves existing patients. Sometimes it is less obvious if a healthcare practitioner owes a person a duty of care and this is the case when the person is not an existing patient of the healthcare practitioner.

With regard to Good Samaritan acts, assuming that the person in need of assistance is a stranger to them, at the point prior to offering their assistance the healthcare practitioner has no duty of care to that individual. Thus, they have no liability if they were to walk away and not offer any assistance.

Before someone can have any liability to another person, from a healthcare perspective, they have to have a duty of care to that person. Therefore, it is necessary to determine whether a healthcare practitioner can assume a duty of care when acting as a Good Samaritan and at what point that duty arises.

When discussing who the duty of care is to earlier in the chapter, it was stated that a duty of care exists when there is a relationship between a healthcare practitioner and a patient, and that the relationship between a healthcare practitioner and a patient is said to exist when the healthcare practitioner assumes responsibility for the patient or for some aspect of their care and treatment.

A healthcare practitioner is said to assume responsibility for a patient when they make the decision to use their skills, knowledge and competence for the benefit of the individuals. As there is no legal duty to assist a member of the public in need of assistance outside of the healthcare practitioner's work environment, the duty of care arises when that healthcare practitioner offers their assistance. At that moment the healthcare practitioner assumes the duty to care for the person and along with that duty the associated liability for their actions.

However, recognising that assuming a liability for their actions could place a healthcare practitioner in the invidious position of being potentially liable if something goes wrong when volunteering to help someone in distress and therefore facing a possible action for negligence. In response to this, the Social Action, Responsibility and Heroism Act 2015 was passed.

4. DUTY OF CARE

The introduction of the Social Action, Responsibility and Heroism Act 2015 requires a judge in a case for negligence in healthcare to ask whether it is reasonable and in the public interests to allow the claim to progress when the healthcare practitioner was acting in a voluntary role during an emergency. The effect of the Act is that it extends the third part of the 3 stage test that originated from Caparo Industries plc v Dickman and others [1990]. You will recall that this is the stage that asks whether it is just and reasonable that a duty of care is imposed on the defendant.

The Social Action, Responsibility and Heroism Act 2015 therefore forms part of a public policy exception to imposing a duty of care on someone where one did not already exist. This allows a healthcare practitioner who voluntarily assists in an emergency a degree of protection from an action for negligence if something were to go wrong.

There are three additional points to note about Good Samaritan acts. The first is that a healthcare practitioner has a duty of care to those patients that are in the care of their employer. Therefore, if a healthcare practitioner were to find a patient collapsed in a hospital corridor they would not be able to just walk on by assuming they had no duty to that patient because he or she was not a patient of theirs. This is because they have a general duty of care. However, that duty of care could be met by calling for assistance from someone who has a better understanding of how to assist the patient. For example, an occupational therapist would have a duty of care to a patient collapsed in a hospital corridor but would not be expected to undertake a full medical assessment to assess what care and treatment they needed or provide full resuscitation on them. Rather calling for assistance and staying with the patient may be the most appropriate action they can take.

The general duty of care a healthcare practitioner has also encompasses relatives and visitors who are on the premises of their employer.

The second point that needs to be made is that although there is no legal obligation on a healthcare practitioner to act as a Good Samaritan, the healthcare regulatory bodies that regulate healthcare practitioners do require them to act. For instance, the Nursing and Midwifery Council's code states that registrants must '*always offer help if an emergency arises in your practice setting or anywhere else*' (Nursing and Midwifery Council 2018 at paragraph 15). Whilst the relevant part of the Health and Care Professions Council code of conduct states that their registrants '*must make sure that your conduct justifies the public's trust and confidence in you and your profession*' (Health and Care Professions Council 2016 at paragraph 9.1). As a final illustration, the General Medical Council's code of conduct states that their registrants '*must offer help in an emergency, taking account of your own safety, your competence, and the availability of other options for care*' (General Medical Council 2024 at paragraph 43).

This means that although there is no legal requirement to do so the healthcare regulatory bodies expect a healthcare practitioner to assume a duty of care and the associated liability that comes with it in an emergency situation.

This raises a question of what standard a healthcare practitioner acting as a Good Samaritan in an emergency is expected to meet so as to fulfil their duty of care. That question is addressed in chapter 5.

The final point to be made about healthcare practitioners and Good Samaritan acts is that as the healthcare practitioner is not working within the scope of their employment, that is they are not working for the benefit of their employer, when they voluntarily assume a duty of care in an emergency situation outside of their place of work, the employer has no vicarious liability for the acts that the healthcare practitioner undertakes. Any liability rests solely with the healthcare practitioner.

Summary of chapter 4

Chapter 4 considered the duty of care aspect of negligence in healthcare.

It is necessary for a claimant to show that a healthcare practitioner owed them a duty of care as the first part of an action for negligence in healthcare. It was noted that the duty of care was established as part of the neighbour principle in the Donoghue v Stevenson [1932] case.

The duty of care was said to be objective in that someone either has a duty or does not. The test for whether a healthcare practitioner owed a duty of care to a specific patient is now based on the 3 stage test from Caparo Industries plc v Dickman and others [1990]. This test is based upon whether it is reasonable for the healthcare practitioner to have a duty of care for the specific patient.

The chapter then moved on to consider who a healthcare practitioner has a duty of care to. It was discussed that for healthcare practitioners it is not so much about whether they have a duty of care, as the law says they do as a result of their special relationship with patients, but more about the scope of that duty.

It was noted that a duty of care is owed if:

- there is an existing relationship between the parties, or
- there is a special relationship between the parties, or
- a reasonable person would foresee that the actions of an individual would affect another person or type of person,

and there is sufficient proximity between the parties meaning it is just and reasonable that a duty of care is imposed on the defendant

The duty of care results in the healthcare practitioner being liable for their actions. Although it can be argued that the duty of care and associated liability is fault based in that it is only relevant if something untoward occurs.

Liability was a considerable part of chapter 4 and various issues in relation to the liability of a healthcare practitioner were considered. These issues included vicarious lability and when someone else can have liability for a healthcare practitioner's actions, including what acting in the course of employment means; the liability of student healthcare practitioners; what indemnity is and when it might be needed by a healthcare practitioner; team liability; and, how liability is affected by delegation.

The chapter concluded by considering Good Samaritan acts and the assumption of both a duty of care and liability by healthcare practitioners.

CHAPTER 5

BREACH OF DUTY AND THE STANDARD OF CARE

Chapter 5 is concerned with breaches of the duty of care. This will involve a discussion of what breach of the duty of care means, the standard by which any alleged breach can be judged and whether there is a specific standard for cases of negligence in healthcare.

As part of the discussion assessing whether a breach of care has occurred the role of expert witnesses in negligence in healthcare cases will be examined.

Following the discussion on breach of the duty of care and the required standard of care there is an exploration of how the standard of care is applied in specific circumstances: such as in emergencies; within healthcare teams; when the healthcare practitioner is a student or otherwise inexperienced; or is an advanced healthcare practitioner; whether there is a team standard for those healthcare practitioners who work as part of a defined team; and how any of these may affect the standard of care and the assessment of whether the duty of care has been breached.

Consideration is also given in chapter 5 to the emergence of evidence based practice, how up to date a healthcare practitioner needs to be, and the role of policies and guidelines in the practice of healthcare practitioners.

Breach of duty

Having established what the duty of care is and when a duty of care is owed in chapter 4, it was noted that this is the first of the four wheels of our milk float. That is a duty of care owed by a healthcare practitioner to a patient is the first of the four elements that have to be proved by a claimant for their negligence in healthcare case to be successful.

Chapter 5 moves our discussion of negligence in healthcare forward by considering the second wheel of the milk float, the second element of negligence in healthcare that a claimant has to prove. This is that the duty of care owed to them by a healthcare practitioner was breached by that healthcare practitioner's actions or omissions.

What is a breach of the duty of care?

As has been stated in the preceding chapters, particularly chapter 3, negligence is concerned with when someone does not act in accordance with how it is reasonable to expect them to act. Specifically in relation to a breach of the duty of care by a healthcare practitioner, if the healthcare practitioner does not act reasonably, and by acting unreasonably the healthcare practitioner has breached their duty of care to their patient.

A breach of the duty of care can therefore be taken to mean that the healthcare practitioners who had a duty of care to the patient did not adequately meet that duty.

A claim for negligence in healthcare will argue that the healthcare practitioner, by breaching the standard of care was at fault. Further that this fault by the healthcare practitioner resulted in harm that was directly caused by the healthcare practitioner's fault in not acting reasonably.

5. BREACH OF DUTY AND THE STANDARD OF CARE

Finding fault is vital in any claim for negligence in healthcare because if there is no fault, even if harm occurred, there can be no negligence.

Harm and causation as to how the fault occurred are discussed in the next two chapters. In this chapter we are just concerned with how a claimant can establish that a healthcare practitioner has breached their duty of care to them.

It has just been stated that a healthcare practitioner breaches their duty of care when they do not act reasonably and thus do not adequately meet their duty of care to a specific patient. Although it is easy to state the duty of care is breached when the duty is not adequately met, there is an assumption in stating that a healthcare practitioner has breached their duty of care, this is that there is a level at which the duty of care has to be delivered. In essence, what is being said is that there is a standard that exists against which the healthcare practitioner's actions can be measured and judged as to whether they were reasonable or not in the circumstances.

This assumption would mean that in a case where a patient is alleging that a healthcare practitioner owed them a duty of care which was subsequently breached by the healthcare practitioner, it would be necessary for the claimant to identify the standard of care that was owed to them under the duty of care and to unfavourably judge the healthcare practitioner's actions against this standard.

This is in fact not just an assumption but a requirement of the process of a claimant establishing, on the balance of probabilities that a healthcare practitioner was negligent in their dealings with them.

Let's just consider this point: in order to determine whether there has been a breach of the duty of care by a healthcare practitioner, it is necessary to identify what the standard of care expected of the healthcare practitioner in the particular set of circumstances is and to assess whether the healthcare practitioner met this required standard. This means that the claimant, or at least their legal representatives, needs to know what the standard of care expected of a healthcare practitioner is.

It also means that in order for us to discuss whether a breach of duty has occurred, we need to consider the standard of care that was applicable to the healthcare practitioner's duty of care in the particular circumstances of the incident that has resulted in a claim for negligence in healthcare.

It is important to note that just because something goes wrong it does not mean that a healthcare practitioner has breached their duty of care to the patient. Things do go wrong, and this can occur through no fault of anyone. A healthcare practitioner only breaches their duty of care when the standard of their practice is below that considered reasonable.

This was confirmed by Lord Denning in Roe v Ministry of Health [1954]. The case concerned a patient who suffered paralysis of the wrist as a result of a contaminated ampoule of a drug. The healthcare practitioner who administered the drug was not found to be negligent because there was no way of knowing that the ampoule had become contaminated.

Lord Denning stated that: *'we must insist on due care for the patient at every point, but we must not condemn as negligence that which is only a misadventure'* (Roe v Ministry of Health [1954] at page 139). This position has been confirmed in subsequent negligence cases.

Therefore, the discussion in the rest of this chapter considers whether a healthcare practitioner has breached their duty of care to a patient by identifying the standard that healthcare

5. BREACH OF DUTY AND THE STANDARD OF CARE

practitioners have to meet to satisfy their liability in relation to their duty of care, and looking at how the standard is met. The next section will begin this discussion by examining the general standard of care.

The general standard of care

In determining a general standard of care for negligence cases the courts have two options. They can either have a general standard that applies in all situations, or they can have multiple general standards that are similar, but each applies in a specific type of situation.

One issue with the latter is that if a novel situation arises then a new general standard of the duty of care will need to be formulated. Another issue is in determining which general standard for the duty of care will apply in a given situation. Although the general standard applies in general cases, the court would need expertise in assisting it to decide if general standard A was to apply or if the specifics of the case meant that general standard B was more appropriate. The more standards there are to cover general cases of negligence, the more complex the situation, and the decision of which of the general standards to apply, becomes more difficult.

It will probably come as no surprise then that the courts have not utilised multiple general standards, but have instead used one standard for general negligence cases that apply in all situations.

In keeping with the development of common law over time, the general standard has evolved as newer cases came before the courts.

The general standard that was applied to cases of negligence to determine if the duty of care had been breached or not was stated in a case we discussed in chapter 3 when considering what negligence is. This was the case of Blythe v Birmingham Water Works Co. (1856).

In that case it was stated that negligence was '*the omission to do something which a reasonable man, guided upon these considerations which ordinarily relate the conduct of human affairs, would do, or doing something which a prudent and reasonable man would not do*' (per Alderson B. in Blyth v Birmingham Water Works Co. (1856) at page 479 -80).

Alderson set a standard for future negligence cases when he stated that based on the facts of the case the defendants in that case '*might have been liable for negligence, if, unintentionally, they omitted to do that which a reasonable person would have done, or did that which a person taking reasonable precautions would not have done*' Blyth v Birmingham Water Works Co. (1856) at page 480).

This resulted in a standard being set based on what is considered to be reasonable in a given situation. With a breach of the duty of care said to have occurred if someone does something that is not considered reasonable or does not do something which it would have been reasonable to do. What is reasonable being assessed as what a reasonable person would do in the same circumstances.

This was an important principle in determining the standard of care as it clearly stated that the test of what was reasonable in a given situation was not a subjective test but rather an objective test. That is, it did not ask what the defendant foresaw or would do (a subjective test) but what a reasonable man would have foreseen or would do (an objective test).

As a consequence of having a general standard based on the objective test of a reasonable person, the notion of a person

5. BREACH OF DUTY AND THE STANDARD OF CARE

to whom the courts could turn to when assessing a claim for negligence became part of the common law.

The problem was in determining who was this reasonable person against which the conduct of all defendants would be assessed and thus the reasonable person who would be able to tell the court what should be done in each and every type of negligence case. That person could best be described as a mythological entity or only present in legal fairy stories.

Over time some characteristics of the reasonable person, often referred as a prudent and reasonable person emerged. This person was of normal intelligence, not a genius but not stupid either. They managed their life in a prudent manner so as not to engage in anything dangerous and considered others. In any given situation they applied reasonable but average skill, they were not the most competent, but neither were they incompetent.

Eventually, in 1932, the reasonable or prudent person test was given a name and became more of an individual that could be recognised. The person became 'the man on the Clapham omnibus'.

This was in the case of Hall v Brooklands Auto-Racing Club [1932]. A case which was concerned with whether a spectator entering premises for a payment to watch a motor race, who was injured when a motor car participating in a race left the track after a collision, was entitled to claim damages under contract law. It was said to be a unique event as no such accident had ever occurred before.

The claimant failed in their claim for two reasons. The first because the danger that occurred was not one that the defendants were legally required to have anticipated, and second because by entering the premises and observing the race the claimant had assumed the risk of such a danger occurring.

Lord Justice Greer had to consider what the terms of a contract were in relation to risk and the safety of spectators. He stated that '*it must be judged by what any reasonable member of the public must have intended should be terms of the contract. The person concerned is sometimes described as "the man in the street," or "the man in the Clapham omnibus"'* (Hall v Brooklands Auto-Racing Club [1932] at page 217).

Although this was a claim in contract law, the case set precedent for future cases where reasonableness of an action needed to be determined by reference to what a reasonable person would do in such circumstances.

An aside: in Hall v Brooklands Auto-Racing Club [1932], Lord Justice Greer made reference to '*the man in the Clapham omnibus*', over time that became changed to the more usable and familiar 'man on the Clapham omnibus'.

The 'man on the Clapham omnibus' as a test for assessing the standard of care in general negligence cases is a very useful one as it allows one test, that of reasonableness, to be used in various different types of situations where negligence is alleged to have occurred. However, there is one issue with the use of the 'man on the Clapham omnibus' test and that is that in order for the test to be applied in a situation it has to be one that the 'man on the Clapham omnibus' would be familiar with.

As noted the 'man on the Clapham omnibus' is a person who uses average skill when assessing the standard that is required in a given situation. Yet there will be situations where the 'man on the Clapham omnibus' does not possess average skill. In these situations, it is not possible or appropriate to use the 'man on the Clapham omnibus' test and another test is needed.

Thus, the 'man on the Clapham omnibus' is unlikely to be someone with the average skills of a healthcare practitioner

5. BREACH OF DUTY AND THE STANDARD OF CARE

and in case of negligence in healthcare another test is needed to assess the standard of care.

It should be noted that in general cases of negligence, the decision of what is reasonable is left to the court in each case using the concept of what they consider the 'man on the Clapham omnibus' would say.

The standard of care in healthcare is discussed in the following section.

As an aside: 1932 was an interesting year for negligence in that the neighbour 'principle' was established in the Donoghue v Stevenson case and the 'man on the Clapham Omnibus' was identified as the individual in the responsible person test in the case of Hall v Brooklands Auto-Racing Club.

The standard of care in healthcare

The 'man on the Clapham Omnibus' as the test to determine the standard of the duty of care is an appropriate test that has stood the test of time where that which is being tested is what is reasonable to expect someone to have done in a given set of circumstances.

However, its suitability can only extend to situations that the 'man on the Clapham Omnibus', or the ordinary person, can understand. This means that its appropriateness is limited to those situations that can be said to fall within general negligence. When the negligence relates to the duty of care of someone who has a special or higher than ordinary level of skill it is outside of the abilities of the 'man on the Clapham Omnibus' to be able to determine what is reasonable in those circumstances.

Thus, another test to determine the standard of care is required for those defendants who have a special or higher than normal skill set that is relevant to their duty of care, and which is called into question in a claim for negligence.

Healthcare practitioners are recognised as one group whose competences and skills are specialist and higher than the ordinary person and thus it is not appropriate for the 'man on the Clapham Omnibus' to be used to assess if their actions were reasonable or not. After all it is unlikely that the 'man on the Clapham Omnibus' is engaged in healthcare practice.

Another reason that a different test is needed rather than using the general standard and the 'man on the Clapham Omnibus' test is that a person who holds themselves out as having a specialist or higher skill set is required to demonstrate that they have a greater level of competence in their practice. Therefore, assessing them against a reasonable person with an ordinary level of skill would not be an adequate test of their competence as they are more than likely going to surpass the competence of the ordinary person.

This would be unfair to a claimant in a case of negligence in healthcare as it would mean that the defendant could demonstrate they have met what would be a lesser standard for them to achieve.

In the introduction we stated that the term healthcare practitioner means someone whose occupation is to provide care and treatment to patients. It includes all those who have a role with patients. Healthcare practitioner does not just mean a single occupation but is a shorthand for all those different occupational groups. Groups such as paramedics, nurses, and physiotherapists.

Some people, including some healthcare practitioners, believe that because of the differences in the practice of the different healthcare practitioner occupational groups there has to be a

5. BREACH OF DUTY AND THE STANDARD OF CARE

different standard of care for each of those occupational groups, rather than a single standard of care and test to assess that standard. This is a reasonable assumption, but it is, in fact, not the case. As with the single test to determine the general standard of care there is one test to determine the standard of care for all healthcare practitioners regardless of their occupation.

That single test originated from a case in 1957. Although over 60 years old it is still the test that is used in cases of negligence in healthcare today, albeit in a modified form.

The case is Bolam v Friern Hospital Management Committee [1957] and the resultant test is known as the 'Bolam test'.

Bolam and reasonableness

The Bolam v Friern Hospital Management Committee [1957] was brought by John Bolam who alleged that he received injuries during a course of electro-convulsive therapy in 1954, due to the negligence of the doctors who administered the electro-convulsive therapy and were employed by Friern Hospital.

A consequence of electro-convulsive therapy is that it causes the patient to have convulsions which can take the form of a seizure or fit during the treatment. Mr Bolam received two electro-convulsive therapy treatments. On neither occasion was Mr Bolam warned by the doctor administering the therapy of the risk associated with electro-convulsive therapy. One risk is that of fracture due to the convulsions.

On the second treatment Mr Bolam was not restrained during the electro-convulsive therapy, neither did he receive a relaxant, which is used to relax the muscles and so reduce the risks associated with the treatment.

During this second treatment Mr Bolam 'sustained severe physical injuries consisting in the dislocation of both hip joints with fractures of the pelvis on each side which were caused by the head of the femur on each side being driven through the acetabulum or cup on the pelvis' (Bolam v Friern Hospital Management Committee [1957] at page 119).

Mr Bolam alleged that the negligence on the second treatment was in administering 'electro-convulsive therapy without the previous administration of a relaxant drug, or without restraining the convulsive movements of the plaintiff by manual control, and in failing to warn the plaintiff of the risk he was taking' (Bolam v Friern Hospital Management Committee [1957] at page 120).

It is worth noting that during the second treatment of electro-convulsive therapy three male nurses were present, as they could have been involved in restraining Mr Bolam. Instead, Mr Bolam *lay in a supine position, a pillow was placed under his back, and his lower jaw was supported on a mouth gag by a male nurse; otherwise he was not restrained in any way*' (Bolam v Friern Hospital Management Committee [1957] at page 119).

The issue for the court was in deciding if the doctor during the second treatment of electro-convulsive therapy had breached their duty of care to Mr Bolam by failing to meet the standard of care required. This required the judge in the case, Mr Justice McNair, to determine what the standard of care was.

A complication in determining the standard of care that was required to meet the duty of care to Mr Bolam was that the defendants did not dispute that using relaxant drugs or manually restraining Mr Bolam would have prevented the risk of fractures occurring. However, they pointed out that both using relaxants and using manual restraint have their own risks associated with them.

There were therefore two schools of thought on the use of relaxants and manual restraint during electro-convulsive

5. BREACH OF DUTY AND THE STANDARD OF CARE

therapy. The defendants stated that they had followed one of these schools of thought.

Mr Justice McNair stated that with regard to negligence *'in the ordinary case which does not involve any special skill, negligence in law means this: some failure to do some act which a reasonable man in the circumstances would do, or doing some act which a reasonable man in the circumstances would not do; and if that failure or doing of that act results in an injury, then there is a cause of action. How do you test if this act or failure is negligent? In an ordinary case it is generally said, that you judge that by the action of the man in the street. He's the ordinary man. In one case it has been said that you judge it by the conduct of the man on top of a Clapham omnibus. He is the ordinary man. But where you get a situation which involves the use of some special skill or competence, then the test whether there has been negligence or not is not the test of the man on top of a Clapham omnibus, because he has not got this special skill. The test is the standard that the ordinary skilled man exercising and professing to have that special skill. A man need not possess the highest expert skill at the risk of being found negligent. It is well established law that it is sufficient if he exercises the ordinary skill of an ordinary competent man exercising that particular art'* (Bolam v Friern Hospital Management Committee [1957] at page 121).

Although Mr Justice McNair has stated the standard that is to be applied in a case involving negligence in healthcare is that of the *'ordinary skilled man exercising and professing to have that special skill'*, given that that any healthcare practitioner could face an allegation of negligence in healthcare, there is a need to substitute the specific occupational group of the defendant healthcare practitioner for 'ordinary skilled man'. This allows a healthcare practitioner, who it is alleged has breached their duty of care, to be judged against the actions of a reasonable healthcare practitioner who has the particular skill relevant to the circumstances. So, if the defendant healthcare practitioner was a nurse, 'ordinary skilled nurse' would be substituted for 'ordinary skilled man', if a paramedic then 'ordinary skilled paramedic' would be the substitution, and so on for the other occupational groups.

A reasonable healthcare practitioner does not have to possess the highest level of skill to meet the required standard of care. It just has to be a reasonable level. What is reasonable is a matter for the courts to decide on a case-by-case basis.

If the defendant healthcare practitioner acted in accordance with what a reasonable healthcare practitioner would have done in the same circumstances then they will have met the standard of care and not breached their duty of care to the patient. Conversely, if the reasonable healthcare practitioner would not have done the same as the defendant healthcare practitioner, then the defendant healthcare practitioner would not have met the standard of care required and they would have breached their duty of care to the patient.

The question of whether a defendant healthcare practitioner has met the required reasonable standard of care is a question of fact that has to be determined in each case of negligence in healthcare using the 'Bolam test'.

An aside: a question of fact is about whether an event happened or whether something met the required level. It is about determining the facts of the case. For instance, it is a question of fact if the four aspects of negligence are proved by the claimant.

A question of law on the other hand is about applying the law to those facts and asking what legal remedy is available to correct the wrong where one has occurred.

5. BREACH OF DUTY AND THE STANDARD OF CARE

Bolam and responsibleness

The fact that there were two opposing views as to whether relaxants and manual restraint should be used during electro-convulsive therapy does not mean that it is not possible to determine the standard that was required in the set of circumstances that resulted in Mr Bolam's injuries.

The Bolam v Friern Hospital Management Committee [1957] case involved a jury and the jury found that the defendants were not negligent.

The reasoning was that Mr Justice McNair gave the jury the direction that '*a doctor is not negligent, if he is acting in accordance with a practice accepted as proper by a responsible body of medical men skilled in that particular art, merely because there is a body of such opinion that takes a contrary view*' (Bolam v Friern Hospital Management Committee [1957] at page 118).

This means that where there are opposing or differing views regarding particular treatment, the defendant has to prove that they used responsible care and skill and acted in accordance with one of the practices that is accepted as proper by a responsible body of medical opinion.

The crucial aspect of Mr Justice McNair's direction to the jury is that '*a doctor is not negligent, if he is acting in accordance with a practice accepted as proper by a responsible body of medical men skilled in that particular art*' Bolam v Friern Hospital Management Committee [1957] at page 118). It is this that has become known as the 'Bolam test' and became the test that is used to determine if a skilled practitioner has met the standard for their duty of care in claims of negligence in healthcare. In cases involving negligence in healthcare, the 'Bolam test' is the second wheel of the milk float.

113

The 'Bolam test' establishes what the standard of practice expected of a healthcare practitioner is in a given set of circumstances. It is to do what others, who share the same skills and competencies, regard as proper practice and thus would have done in the same circumstances.

The standard of care is to provide reasonable care, with what is considered reasonable to be decided by application of the 'Bolam test'.

As noted earlier, it is a question of fact in each case for the court to determine if the defendant did in fact act in accordance with a responsible body of medical opinion.

If a claimant is not able to prove that the healthcare practitioner breached their duty of care based on the 'Bolam test', their claim will fail at that point.

A few points about the 'Bolam test'

- The 'Bolam test' is worded in terms of doctors and medical men, that was the language of the time, but the test applies to all healthcare practitioners regardless of their occupational group and irrespective of whether they are men or not
- It is not sufficient for a claimant to establish that there is a responsible body of opinion which disagrees with the actions of the defendant healthcare practitioner, if there is also a responsible body of opinion which supports the defendant's actions
- Therefore, a defendant healthcare practitioner is not negligent simply because they did something different if it is judged that they used reasonable and responsible skill and competence
- The 'Bolam test' means that healthcare practitioners are judged against the practice of other healthcare

5. BREACH OF DUTY AND THE STANDARD OF CARE

practitioners to determine whether they have met the standard of care necessary
- Whilst the duty of care is imposed by law, see chapter 4 for the discussion relating to this, the standard of care is a matter for the various healthcare occupations as it is they who determine what is responsible practice or not
- Cases of negligence in healthcare take some time to come to court. In the Bolam v Friern Hospital Management Committee [1957] case the event happened in August 1954, but the case was heard in February 1957. In the intervening years accepted practices can change. It is therefore important to consider what standard of care should be applied; it is the responsible practice at the time of the event and not at the time of the court hearing that should be used. This was noted by Lord Denning when he stated that although the defendants in the case were not negligent at the time of an incident in 1947, if the incident had happened at the time of the trial in 1954 they almost certainly would have been found negligent as responsible practice had changed considerably. In Denning's words *'we must not look at the 1947 accident with 1954 spectacles'* (Roe v Ministry of Health [1954] at page 137)
- The standard that the defendant healthcare practitioner has to achieve is that of the ordinary healthcare practitioner who has the necessary skills. The defendant healthcare practitioner does not need to demonstrate the highest level of skill to meet the standard. However, they have to be at least ordinary, so having the lowest level of skill, that is below average, would not meet the standard

Expert witnesses

Using the 'Bolam test' means that the court has to judge if a defendant healthcare practitioner had achieved the standard necessary for them to have met their duty of care to the patient. As judges cannot be said to be skilled in healthcare practice the 'Bolam test' requires the court to have expert witnesses.

Expert witnesses are healthcare practitioners, normally from the same occupational group as the defendant healthcare practitioner, who, in the words of Mr Justice McNair, profess to have the *special skill* that the defendant healthcare practitioner claims to have. That is, expert witnesses are from the professions that normally undertake the activity that is said to have resulted in the negligence. Their role is to provide evidence to the judge upon which they may base their decision as to whether the standard of care was met or breached.

The expert witnesses represent the responsible body of opinion.

Expert witnesses are appointed to the court, and they are responsible to the court and are appointed as independent witnesses to the court. In some cases of negligence in healthcare the breach of the duty of care is not in question and both the claimant and the defendant accept that it was breached, and the case is to be decided on the issue of, for example, causation.

However, generally there is a dispute over standards that should have been followed and both the claimant and the defendant will have their own expert witnesses to advise them on whether the defendant's duty of care was breached by their failure to meet the required standard.

There is often more than one way of caring for and treating a patient. It is the job of expert witnesses to advise the court as to what a reasonable and responsible body of practitioners skilled in the particular practice of the defendant healthcare practitioner would have done in the same circumstances. Also, whether the specific actions that the healthcare practitioner

5. BREACH OF DUTY AND THE STANDARD OF CARE

took were reasonable and met the required standard, especially where there is more than one approach that could have been used by the healthcare practitioner.

Expert witnesses do this by reviewing the evidence and writing reports on the standard the patient was entitled to expect and how that compares with what took place. They may also be asked to attend court to give their opinion directly to the judge.

Just for clarity, although the evidence of the expert witness is taken into account when a judgment is made in a specific case, it is the judge(s) in the case that make the judgment not the expert witnesses.

Developments since the establishment of the Bolam test

The 'Bolam test' was established as the test to determine if a healthcare practitioner has met their duty of care to a patient in 1957. That is some 60+ years ago. Much has changed in both the law and in healthcare practice during those 60+ years.

Yet, the 'Bolam test' is still the legal test used to determine the standard of care in cases of negligence in healthcare to this day. It has been approved in several cases since it was first established, that is later cases have stated that it is the correct test to use for cases involving negligence in healthcare.

That is not to say that there has not been criticism of the 'Bolam test'. Some of the criticisms levelled at the use of the 'Bolam test' include:

- It is not an objective test of the defendant healthcare practitioner as their actions are effectively judged by other healthcare practitioners who act as the reasonable and responsible body of practitioners skilled in the particular

NEGLIGENCE IN HEALTHCARE

practice of the defendant healthcare practitioner. Thus making it a subjective test. This is sometime referred to as the law imposing the duty of care but the standard of care being decided by healthcare practitioners themselves

- Allied to this, it has been said that the 'Bolam test' works without the input of Judges as it is the healthcare practitioners who are setting the standard and determining if a defendant healthcare practitioner's practice passes the test and thus meets the required standard
- That the 'Bolam test' results in a form of paternalism in that by using expert witnesses from the defendant healthcare practitioner's own occupational group it is essentially a form of 'doctor knows best' because the same occupational group is saying what standard of care the patient was entitled to expect
- It puts judges in the position of having to decide between expert witnesses when they disagree on the standard of care the defendant healthcare practitioner should have achieved to meet their duty of care to the patient
- It is not appropriate to judge the actions of defendant healthcare practitioners who undertake experimental treatment or are so advanced in their practice that there is not a responsible body of healthcare practitioners who practise in that area. Therefore, there is no-one who can act as an expert witnesses and provide a responsible opinion as to what the standard of care should be and whether the defendant healthcare practitioner met their duty of care to the patient

With regard to judges deciding between expert witnesses with differing views on what the appropriate standard of care should have been, a 1985 case established that judges do not have to decide between competing expert opinions.

5. BREACH OF DUTY AND THE STANDARD OF CARE

Maynard v West Midlands Regional Health Authority [1985] concerned a woman who was thought to be suffering from tuberculosis but may also have had Hodgkin's disease. Two consultants decided to perform an exploratory operation to determine if she did indeed have Hodgkin's disease. The operation was undertaken by one of the consultants and confirmed that the woman was in fact suffering with tuberculosis and not Hodgkin's disease. However, during the operation a nerve to the woman's vocal cords was damaged causing her speech to be impaired.

Mrs Maynard sued for negligence in carrying out the operation in the first place and not waiting for the result of a tuberculosis test to come back and secondly for the resultant damage and impairment of her speech.

Expert evidence was provided by both sides and in the original case the judge preferred Mrs Maynard's expert's opinion. The defendants appealed to the Court of Appeal and the decision was reversed stating that there had been no negligence. The case then went to the House of Lords.

In reaching their decision, which was for the defendants, Lord Scarman noted that *'a judge's 'preference' for one body of distinguished professional opinion to another also professionally distinguished is not sufficient to establish negligence in a practitioner whose actions have received the seal of approval of those whose opinions, truthfully expressed, honestly held, were not preferred. If this was the real reason for the judge's finding, he erred in law even though elsewhere in his judgment he stated the law correctly. For in the realm of diagnosis and treatment negligence is not established by preferring one respectable body of professional opinion to another. Failure to exercise the ordinary skill of a doctor (in the appropriate speciality, if he be a specialist) is necessary'*

(Maynard v West Midlands Regional Health Authority [1985] at page 639).

What Lord Scarman said is that a judge is not in a position to choose between two differing yet responsible expert opinions and therefore should not do so. If one of the opinions expressed supports the defendant's actions then this is enough to find that the defendant has not breached their duty of care to the patient.

The reason that the defendants were not found to have been negligent is that using the 'Bolam test' identified that there was a body of responsible opinion which determined that their actions were reasonable and met the required standard. A defendant is only to be found negligent if they are judged not to have met the standard of a responsible body of opinion as determined through use of the 'Bolam test'.

Introducing an element of logic into the 'Bolam test'

The issue that arises from Maynard v West Midlands Regional Health Authority [1985], in relation to the standard of care, is that there can be a responsible body of opinion that either supports the defendant's actions that is not sensible and/or does not have a logical basis. However, as it is being presented by a responsible body of opinion the 'Bolam test' is passed and the defendant healthcare practitioner would not be found to have committed a negligent act. This was in fact the situation in the case of Bolitho v City & Hackney Health Authority [1997].

The case concerned Patrick Bolitho a 2 year old boy who had been readmitted to hospital with croup. The day after his admission Patrick had two episodes of croup which resulted in him having breathing difficulties. A doctor Horn was called but she delegated Dr Rodger, her junior, to attend instead.

5. BREACH OF DUTY AND THE STANDARD OF CARE

Neither in fact attended and a short while later Patrick suffered a respiratory and cardiac arrest and died.

The case was brought by Patrick's mother as administratrix of his estate, alleging negligence. The breach of the duty of care owed to Patrick was established but the issue of causation was the central issue to be decided.

The question that needed answering was, would Patrick have avoided the cardiac arrest which led to his death if he had been intubated on either of the two times he suffered croup earlier in the day?

This was a crucial question because if Dr Horn would have intubated Patrick then her failure to do so would have caused Patrick's death. If she would not have intubated Patrick then the failure did not cause his death, unless not doing so was not in keeping with a responsible body of opinion.

Dr Horn stated that she would not have intubated Patrick even if she had attended him and in total 8 expert witnesses gave evidence. Five were instructed by the claimant and stated they would have intubated Patrick and 3 were instructed by the defendants and said that they would not have intubated Patrick.

The original trial judge used the judgment from the Maynard v West Midlands Regional Health Authority [1985] case in not choosing between opposing views of experts and applying the 'Bolam test' noted that there was a responsible body of opinion supporting the defendants and thus they were not negligent.

The claimant took the case to the Court of Appeal who upheld the original decision. The House of Lords also heard an appeal from the claimant but on the facts held that there had been no negligence.

However, Lord Browne-Wilkinson's judgment included an important point in relation to the use of the 'Bolam test'. He stated that a *'court is not bound to hold that a defendant doctor escapes liability for negligent treatment or diagnosis just because he leads evidence from a number of medical experts who are genuinely of the opinion that the defendant's treatment or diagnosis accorded with sound medical practice. ... the court has to be satisfied that the exponents of the body of opinion relied on can demonstrate that such opinion has a logical basis. ...the judge before accepting a body of opinion as being responsible, reasonable or respectable, will need to be satisfied that, in forming their views, the experts have directed their minds to the question of comparative risks and benefits and have reached a defensible conclusion on the matter'* (Bolitho v City & Hackney Health Authority [1997] at page 778).

This is an important statement because it is saying that even if there is expert opinion which supports a defendant's actions such that the 'Bolam test' would be a passed, a judge can still find that the defendant has been negligent if the body of opinion cannot logically defend those opinions.

This put the decision as to whether a defendant has reached the standard of care back with the judge, as it requires them to consider if opinion is logical i.e. capable of withstanding logical scrutiny.

Lord Browne-Wilkinson did note that *'it will very seldom be right for a judge to reach the conclusion that views genuinely held by a competent medical expert are unreasonable. The assessment of medical risks and benefits is a matter of clinical judgment which a judge would not normally be able to make without expert evidence'* (Bolitho v City & Hackney Health Authority [1997] at page 779). Effectively saying that although

5. BREACH OF DUTY AND THE STANDARD OF CARE

a judge is able set aside expert opinions if it considers that they are not able to withstand logical scrutiny, it should not be a common occurrence.

A qualified 'Bolam test'

The 'Bolam test' has been qualified, or modified, by the judgment in the Bolitho v City & Hackney Health Authority [1997] case. Although we still refer to the 'Bolam test', if we were being pedantic, and if you can't be pedantic when talking about the law when can you be, it should really be called the 'Bolam test as modified by the principles in Bolitho' or even just the 'Bolitho test'. But 'Bolam test' it remains!

The revised 'Bolam test', is essentially a two stage test, or a double opportunity for a claimant to establish that a defendant healthcare practitioner has breached their duty of care.

The first stage or opportunity is that of the original aspect of the 'Bolam test', determining if the defendant has acted in accordance with a responsible body of opinion. If the defendant hasn't then the claimant has proved this aspect of the case and can move on to proving they have suffered harm and that the breach of the duty of care by the defendant caused the harm.

If, however, the defendant can establish that they acted in accordance with a responsible body of opinion the second stage or opportunity asks if that responsible body of opinion is able to withstand logical scrutiny.

If it isn't then the claimant will have proved that the defendant breached their duty of care to them. If the responsible body of opinion does withstand logical scrutiny then the defendant will have proved that they met their duty of care to the claimant, and the claimant will have been unsuccessful in their claim for negligence in healthcare.

The 'Bolam test' now requires not only that healthcare practitioner's practice is in keeping with the accepted practice as defined by a responsible body of opinion but also that their practice can stand up to logical analysis, in order to be deemed to have met the standard of care.

A modification on the 'Bolam test'

As a result of the modification of the 'Bolam test' by the judgment in Bolitho v City & Hackney Health Authority [1997], a number of the criticisms levelled at the 'Bolam test' can be said to have been addressed, at least in part.

The 'Bolam test' is now an objective test, as whilst the reasonable and responsible body of practitioners skilled in the particular practice of the defendant healthcare practitioner is still relevant and important, their opinion is tempered by the fact that it has to withstand logical scrutiny.

Judges are vital to the workings of the 'Bolam test' as it is they who will decide if an expert opinion is capable of withstanding logical scrutiny. It is the judgment of the court that matters in determining if a defendant has met the standard for their duty of care.

The doctor, or any other healthcare practitioner, will only know best if they practise in a way that is in accordance with a responsible body of opinion and has a logical basis.

A healthcare practitioner can undertake experimental treatment or depart from accepted healthcare practice if they use a reasonable and logical basis to do so.

The modified 'Bolam test' has been referred to as a patient centred approach as it requires the healthcare practitioner to consider what is the logical basis for treating the patient in front of them in a certain way. It is no longer possible to just point to

5. BREACH OF DUTY AND THE STANDARD OF CARE

a responsible body of opinion and say that is why I am treating the patient this way, if that way has no logical basis to it. The specific circumstances of the actual patient have to be considered to determine whether they affect the treatment they receive. This includes the information that a patient receives regarding the treatment as well, so that they may make an informed decision. You will recall the lack of information given to Mr Bolam was part of the claim for negligence in the Bolam v Friern Hospital Management Committee [1957] case.

On the issue of disclosing information to patients the Pearce v United Bristol Healthcare NHS Trust (1998) is important. The case was concerned with whether a consultant should have advised a woman that a delay in delivering her baby would lead to an increased risk of still birth, which in fact occurred.

Although the consultant was not deemed to be negligent as it was considered that the woman would not have acted upon the information, Lord Woolf stated that '*if there is a significant risk which would affect the judgment of a reasonable patient, then in the normal course it is the responsibility of a doctor to inform the patient of the significant risk, if the information is needed so that the patient can determine for him or herself what course he or she should adopt*' (Pearce v United Bristol Healthcare NHS Trust (1998) at page 124).

The judgment in the Maynard v West Midlands Regional Health Authority [1985] case regarding a judge not being in a position to choose between two differing yet responsible expert opinions and therefore should not do so, still applies to cases of negligence in healthcare. However, as a consequence of Bolitho v City & Hackney Health Authority [1997] a judge can decide that an expert opinion does not withstand logical scrutiny.

An aside: It used to be thought, by some healthcare practitioners and lawyers specialising in this area of law, that all a defendant healthcare practitioner had to do to successfully defend their actions was to produce an expert witness who would support those actions. With the requirement that the responsible body of opinion has to be capable of withstanding logical scrutiny this is no longer the case.

Evidence based practice

Evidence based practice existed before the Bolitho v City & Hackney Health Authority [1997] case but it can be said that the requirement that a healthcare practitioner's standard of care has a logical basis was a contributory factor to the acceptance of evidence-based practice within healthcare.

According to Sackett et al (1996) *'Evidence based medicine is the conscientious, explicit, and judicious use of current best evidence in making decisions about the care of individual patients. The practice of evidence-based medicine means integrating individual clinical expertise with the best available external clinical evidence from systematic research'* (at page 71).

Essentially evidence-based practice requires a healthcare practitioner to consider their practice and question why they are doing something and what is the reason that they choose one course of action over another. The reasoning should be because the available evidence supports that particular course of action in the specific circumstances that the healthcare practitioner is working within.

Evidence based practice is a way of healthcare practitioners making decisions about their own practice using their individual expertise and clinical judgment aligned with the best available evidence.

The evidence used should provide an indication of what best practice is regarding a particular healthcare condition or a

5. BREACH OF DUTY AND THE STANDARD OF CARE

specific treatment option. Allowing the healthcare practitioner to decide what is the most appropriate treatment for their patient's condition.

The relationship between evidence-based practice and the standard of care is that evidence-based practice can be seen as a form of quality assurance mechanism as if a healthcare practitioner is using the best available evidence to inform their practice they should be providing effective clinical practice for their patients. Using evidence-based practice would mean that the healthcare practitioner can defend their practice, if needed, by indicating the evidence they have used and highlighting how they have used this to provide a logical basis upon which they make their clinical decisions. Thus, they would be showing how they meet the 'Bolam test' and therefore how they achieve the required standard of care in their duty to their patients.

Keeping up to date

In order to be able to use evidence to inform their practice healthcare practitioners need to be aware of the evidence that exists. This requires healthcare practitioners to keep up to date with developments in their area of speciality. Otherwise, they may not be aware of a new piece of evidence which details a more effective approach to an aspect of their practice. After all, evidence-based practice is about the conscientious use of the current best evidence to inform clinical decision making.

This begs the question of how up to date a healthcare practitioner needs to be.

All the codes of conduct issued by the healthcare regulatory bodies make reference to the need for their respective registrants to keep up to date. As an example of what is expected by a healthcare regulatory body, the Nursing and Midwifery Council's code states that registrants must 'keep your knowledge and skills up to date, taking part in appropriate and regular learning and professional development activities that aim to maintain and develop your competence and improve your performance' (Nursing and Midwifery Council 2018 at paragraph 22.3).

Although highlighting that keeping up to date is a requirement of being registered with a healthcare regulatory body, it doesn't answer the question of how up to date a healthcare practitioner needs to be.

The answer as to how up to date a healthcare practitioner needs to be in order to meet the standard of care of their practice actually lies in the standard of care itself. Apologies if this is going to sound like a circular argument but bear with us.

Healthcare practitioners have to keep up to date in order for their practice to be appropriate and effective for their patients. They have both a regulatory and a legal duty to do so and this is reflected in the standard of care. The standard of a healthcare practitioner's practice is judged against the standard of care which, as this chapter has discussed, is assessed by the 'Bolam test'. This requires the healthcare practitioner's practice to be judged against a reasonable body of opinion that can be logically defended. Essentially is the healthcare practitioner practising in the same way as their fellow healthcare practitioners and is there a logical basis for the way they practise.

As the reason that the healthcare practitioner is keeping up to date is in relation to their practice the same standard must be applied to keeping up to date as to any other aspect of their practice. Thus, the 'Bolam test' is the way of assessing if a healthcare practitioner is keeping as up to date as they need to be. Essentially measuring them against their fellow healthcare practitioners.

5. BREACH OF DUTY AND THE STANDARD OF CARE

Although there will be a minimum standard for keeping up to date, that is the minimum that it is logically defendable to do. This has to be a reasonable expectation of what healthcare practitioners are able to do. So, we can expect a healthcare practitioner to keep themselves abreast of the latest evidence and treatments that are important to their practice, and to know their local guidelines and be aware of major changes in practice within their area of expertise. However, we cannot expect an ordinary healthcare practitioner to be aware of every piece of evidence and to know everything that is in all the journals pertinent to their area of practice.

Policies & guidelines

Various organisations produce policies and guidelines for healthcare practice. Some of these will be national organisations such as Royal Colleges and the Department of Health, while others may be more local to a healthcare practitioner, such as their employer. Thus, a policy may apply nationally to all healthcare practitioners or may only apply to those who are members of a particular occupational group, or those who work within a particular locality, or for a specific employer.

It may be thought that in order for healthcare practitioners to meet the standard of care they would have to follow all policies and guidelines relevant to their area of practice. After all, healthcare policies and guidelines are in effect a form of standard that establishes accepted practice, or a minimum level of competency required from a healthcare practitioner in their practice.

However, there is no legal requirement for a healthcare practitioner to follow a policy or guideline, if in their professional judgment they believe that there is a valid logical reason not to do so. For instance, if they believe that there may be an issue with a specific policy or guideline in relation to their practice or their patient.

Examples of these issues include that the policy or guideline may be out of date, they may contain incorrect information, they may contain information that conflicts with another policy or guidance, or they may not be appropriate for certain categories of patient. Some policies and guidelines contain information that is general, and whilst appropriate for the majority of patients there may be a small number of patients for whom it is inappropriate. If a healthcare practitioner was aware that the information in a guideline was not appropriate for their patient but followed it anyway, this in itself could be seen as breaching the standard of care.

The one exception to a healthcare practitioner deciding whether to follow a policy or guideline is the guidance issued by the healthcare regulatory bodies. This is taken as the standard of care and so it would be extremely rare that a healthcare practitioner could have a logically defensible reason for not adhering to the code of conduct issued by their healthcare regulatory body.

If a healthcare practitioner does not follow a policy or guideline they will need to prove that they still met the required standard in their duty of care to their patient by showing that their decision not to follow it in the specific circumstances is supported by a reasonable and responsible body of opinion and that this was a logical decision to make. That is, that they can satisfy the requirements of the 'Bolam test' in relation to that decision.

On the other hand, where a healthcare practitioner does follow a policy or guideline and something goes wrong as a consequence of them doing so, the fact that they adhered to that policy or guideline will likely be a defence against a claim of negligence in healthcare.

This was the situation a healthcare practitioner faced in the case of Cowley v Cheshire and Merseyside Strategic Health Authority (2007). The case was concerned with whether a woman was in premature labour or not and if she should have received a specific medication. The claimant alleged that if she had received the medication her son would not have been born with brain damage.

The policy of the hospital was that if on examination the woman was not in active premature labour the drug should not be given. The doctor who examined the woman did not consider the woman to be in premature labour and so the drug was not administered.

The woman was unsuccessful in her claim for negligence in healthcare because the doctor had followed the local policy and because the policy had a logical basis to it the doctor had therefore met their duty of care to her.

Emergencies and the standard of care

The question that this section is seeking to answer is whether there a different standard that is applied in emergencies.

There are two forms of emergency that we will consider. The first is an emergency within a healthcare environment and the send is an emergency outside of the healthcare environment.

Emergencies within a healthcare environment

Healthcare practitioners may be faced by an emergency situation because a patient's condition has become critical, and something needs to be done immediately. In this situation the normal standard of care still applies, the 'Bolam test' will be applied to the actions of the healthcare practitioners involved to determine if they have met the standard of care they owed to the patient.

Another form of emergency may occur when the clinical unit is overwhelmed by the needs of multiple patients. Either there are not enough healthcare practitioners or there are not enough resources to provide the treatment that the patients need. An example would be a major incident at a hospital where there is a sudden influx of patients all requiring immediate care.

It was this latter situation that Lord Justice Mustill had in mind in the Wilsher v Essex Area Health Authority [1986]. The facts of the case are outlined in chapter 4 in the decision on team liability.

What is pertinent about the case in relation to the standard of care in an emergency are the remarks made by Lord Justice Mustill. He remarked that *'full allowance must be made for the fact that certain aspects of treatment may have to be carried out in what one witness ... called "battle conditions". An emergency may overburden the available resources, and, if an individual is forced by circumstances to do too many things at once, the fact he does one of them incorrectly should not lightly be taken as negligence'* (Wilsher v Essex Area Health Authority [1986] at page 812).

Lord Justice Mustill has not said that there is a lower standard of care that needs to be applied to the emergency situation. What he has said is that the standard that the healthcare practitioner is assessed against is that of a healthcare practitioner in an emergency situation, not on a normal calm day.

This would mean that if something happened during an emergency situation the 'Bolam test' would still be applied to the actions of the healthcare practitioners involved but the responsible body of opinion would be based upon acting in an emergency situation and not what would be expected in a non-emergency situation. This is sometimes referred to as the standard of care not being fixed, but adapting to

5. BREACH OF DUTY AND THE STANDARD OF CARE

the circumstances in which the healthcare practitioner finds themselves.

Emergencies outside a healthcare environment

This form of emergency was discussed in chapter 4 in the section on Good Samaritans. There it was noted that a healthcare practitioner has no legal duty to assist outside of their work environment unless they have an existing duty of care to the person in need of assistance. Where it was also noted that they do have a duty to act as a result of their registration with a healthcare regulatory body, which requires them to act to assist anyone in need of their services unless it puts them in danger.

It was also noted that if they do act as a Good Samaritan they will assume liability for their actions.

However, whilst they will have a duty of care and the standard for assessing if they have met that duty will be the 'Bolam test' the standard will be adjusted to take account of their normal competencies. This means that if a physiotherapist were to stop to assist at a roadside collision, they would not be expected to operate at the competence of a trauma doctor or a paramedic but the competencies of a physiotherapist in an unfamiliar situation.

Returning to Lord Justice Mustill, he stated that if a healthcare practitioner '*assumes to perform a task, he must bring to it the appropriate care and skill. What the courts can do, however, is to bear constantly in mind that, in those situations which call for the exercise of judgment, the fact that in retrospect the choice actually made can be shown to have turned out badly is not in itself a proof of negligence, and to remember that the duty of care is not a warranty of a perfect result*' (Wilsher v Essex Area Health Authority [1986] at page 810).

Although the healthcare practitioner acting as a Good Samaritan would do well to remember that if they act outside of their normal competence and were to do things that only the trauma doctor or paramedic would do they will be assuming the higher standard on themselves.

This means that healthcare practitioners should work to their own competencies, which may mean that the assistance they provide is at the level of caring and not treating and in calling for further assistance, e.g. by telephoning the emergency services.

Therefore, it can be seen that in either type of emergency the standard of care that is required remains the same and is assessed by the 'Bolam test', but the difference is that the level of that standard takes account of the fact that the healthcare practitioner is working within an emergency situation.

The standard for juniors and trainees/students

The liability of junior and student members of the healthcare team was discussed in chapter 4, where it was stated that they have their own liability and are not protected by virtue of being a junior or student member of the healthcare team.

Now, we are sure you are thinking, yes they are liable for their own actions but the standard they have to achieve is a lower standard than that for their qualified and more experienced colleagues. Maybe your aren't thinking that but a majority of our students do ask us that!

Three cases are relevant to determine the standard of care that is used to determine if a junior or student healthcare practitioner has met their duty of care.

Taking the cases in the order they were heard, the first case we need to consider is that of Jones v Manchester Corporation [1952]. In this case a junior doctor gave a drug that they were unfamiliar with to a patient without any supervision and without

5. BREACH OF DUTY AND THE STANDARD OF CARE

discussing it with a more experienced colleague. The patient died because the drug given interacted with other drugs they were receiving.

In his judgment in the case Lord Justice Denning declared that *'errors due to inexperience or lack of supervision are no defence against the injured person'*, (Jones v Manchester Corporation [1952] at page 871).

The second case for us to consider is a non-healthcare related one. The case of Nettleship v Weston [1971] concerned Weston, a learner motor car driver, and a friend, Nettleship, acting as an instructor. When Nettleship suffered a broken kneecap as a result of Weston hitting a lamp post during a driving lesson, he sued her for negligence.

One of the issues in the case was the standard expected of Mrs Weston as a learner driver.

Lord Denning made several observations in his judgment that are relevant to our discussion. He noted that Mrs Weston could have said, *'I was a learner driver under instruction. I was doing my best and could not help it'*, however he noted that would not suffice as *'every person driving a car must attain an objective standard measured by the standard of a skilled, experienced and careful driver'* (Nettleship v Weston [1971] at page 585).

He went on to say that *'the learner-driver may be doing his best, but his incompetent best is not good enough'* (Nettleship v Weston [1971] at page 586).

When discussing whether there should be different standards for different classes of individual, Lord Justice Megaw stated that *'the certainty of a general standard is preferable to the vagaries of a fluctuating standard'* (Nettleship v Weston [1971] at page 592).

The court found that Mrs Weston was therefore negligent.

We have already discussed the Wilsher v Essex Area Health Authority [1986] in this chapter when looking at the standard of care in the emergency situation. However, the judgment in that case is also relevant to the standard of care that is applied to junior and student healthcare practitioners.

Lord Justice Glidewell when discussing whether there should be a lesser standard for the newly qualified healthcare practitioners stated that '*in my view, the law requires the trainee or learner to be judged by the same standard as his more experienced colleagues. If he did not, inexperience would frequently be urged as a defence to an action for professional negligence*', (Wilsher v Essex Area Health Authority [1986] at page 831).

The precedent in all three of these cases says the same: inexperience is no excuse in law. The standard of care for a junior or student healthcare practitioner is the same as their qualified more experience colleague. Further, the junior or student healthcare practitioner will be assessed using the same test as that of their qualified more experienced colleagues: the 'Bolam test'.

If it sems unfair that a junior or student healthcare practitioner is held to the same standard as other healthcare practitioners, there are two points to be made.

The first is that the standard to which they are being held is that of the 'Bolam test', and in the words of Mr Justice McNair '*a doctor is not negligent, if he is acting in accordance with a practice accepted as proper by a responsible body of medical men skilled in that particular art*' Bolam v Friern Hospital Management Committee [1957] at page 118).

We know that this means that a particular healthcare practitioner is to be assessed against other healthcare practitioners who have the same role as the one being assessed. This means

5. BREACH OF DUTY AND THE STANDARD OF CARE

that a junior healthcare practitioner would be assessed against a responsible body of junior healthcare practitioners, and a student healthcare practitioner would be assessed against a responsible body of student healthcare practitioners.

The second point is eloquently put by Lord Justice Glidewell when he addressed whether it was harsh to subject the inexperienced healthcare practitioner to the same standard and test as their experienced colleagues. He said: *'I should add that, in my view, the inexperienced doctor called on to exercise a specialist skill will, as part of that skill, seek the advice and help of his superiors when he does or may need it. If he does seek such help, he will have satisfied the test, even though he may himself have made a mistake'* (Wilsher v Essex Area Health Authority [1986] at page 831).

Thus, a junior or student healthcare practitioner can discharge their duty and hence meet the required standard expected of them by contacting someone senior for advice, as that is what a responsible junior or student healthcare practitioner would do.

Advanced Practitioners: the standard for specialist or special skills

For the purposes of this discussion, we are going to use the term advanced practitioner to mean a healthcare practitioner who has expanded their role and has skills and expertise above that of the ordinary level of healthcare practitioner in that occupational group. There are various terms and job/role titles that are used for healthcare practitioners who expand their practice, but we will stick with advanced practitioner as a form of shorthand for all of them.

Because they have these specialist skills and expertise it is necessary to clarify if advanced practitioners have the same standard as the other healthcare practitioners in their occupational group or whether a different standard applies to them.

This is especially so when the advanced practitioner expands their role into areas that were traditionally the preserve of other healthcare practitioner occupational groups. For instance, the nurse or paramedic who takes over activities that were undertaken by doctors.

There are two cases which assist us with determining the standard of care required for advanced practitioners. The first is Maynard v West Midlands Regional Health Authority [1985].

This case was described when we were discussing 'Developments since the establishment of the Bolam test'. As well as providing precedent concerning judges not being in a position to choose between two differing yet responsible expert opinions and therefore should not do so. The judgment in the case is also relevant to the standard of care that is required for healthcare practitioners with specialist or special skills, the advanced practitioner.

In Maynard v West Midlands Regional Health Authority [1985] Lord Scarman stated that '*a doctor who professes to exercise a special skill must exercise the ordinary skill of his speciality*' (at page 638).

The second case that assists us may sound counterintuitive, but it is the one we used previously when answering the question of whether a junior or student healthcare practitioner should have a lower standard of care to meet than their more experienced colleagues. This is the Wilsher v Essex Area Health Authority [1986] case.

Lord Justice Mustill gave two opinions in his judgments in the Wilsher v Essex Area Health Authority [1986] case that explain the standard of care required of an advanced practitioner. The

5. BREACH OF DUTY AND THE STANDARD OF CARE

first was '*to my mind, this notion of a duty tailored to the actor, rather than to the act which he elects to perform, has no place in the law or tort*', whilst the second is that '*the duty of care* [is related], *not to the individual, but to the post which he occupies*' (Wilsher v Essex Area Health Authority [1986] at page 813).

The judgments from both of these cases say the same thing: if a healthcare practitioner takes on additional roles as an advanced practitioner, then their patients can expect them to achieve the same standard of care that they could have expected from the healthcare practitioner who would previously have undertaken that role or task. It is not who has undertaken the task that is important in determining the standard of care but what role the task falls within that is the determining factor.

For the advanced healthcare practitioner this means that the expansion of their role into advanced practice using specialist or special skills will result in them having an increased or greater liability. This greater liability is not an additional liability but is said to be increased because although they are still assessed according to the 'Bolam test', the responsible body of opinion will come not from their own occupational group but from members of the occupational group that formerly undertook those activities that the advanced practitioner has assumed.

Therefore, we can say that the standard of care required of an advanced practitioner is based on who formerly undertook that role or activity. Those that they are replacing. Although it must be remembered that some advanced practitioners are undertaking tasks that are still undertaken by other healthcare practitioners, and so they are not replacing them but acting alongside them in their advanced role.

In short, if an activity is one that a doctor does or did do then the performance of the activity will be judged by the standard performance of a responsible doctor.

For the healthcare practitioner who is considering becoming an advanced practitioner this means that they need to consider the scope of the advanced role, the competence of that role and whether they have the competencies and skills to adequately perform at the level of an advanced practitioner.

A team standard?

The concept of collective team liability was discussed in chapter 4 where it was noted that team liability is not recognised in law. That each individual member of a team is individually liable for their actions.

In a similar way there is no recognition of a team standard of care. This was confirmed by Lord Justice Mustill in the Wilsher v Essex Area Health Authority [1986] case when he stated that '*it cannot be right, for it would expose a student nurse to an action in negligence for failure to possess the skill and experience of a consultant*' (at page 813).

Each member of the healthcare team will have the standard of their duty of care assessed by a responsible body of their occupational group, unless they are practising in an advanced role, as discussed earlier. This means that if a healthcare team comprises a physiotherapist, a nurse, and a doctor, the physiotherapist would have their standard of care assessed by a responsible body of physiotherapists, the nurse by a responsible body of nurses, and the doctor by a responsible body of doctors. All would be assessed according to the 'Bolam test'.

The only way that the assessment of the standard of care would be affected by teamwork is that the responsible body of opinion would have to consider the ability of the healthcare practitioner to be a team member and to fulfil the functions of a team member. This may, for instance, include their skills in

5. BREACH OF DUTY AND THE STANDARD OF CARE

communicating to other members of the team and their ability to understand their role within the team and to stay within the boundaries of their role and not encroach on the role of others.

Summary of chapter 5

Chapter 5 has been concerned with how a breach of the duty of care owed by a healthcare practitioner to a patient can be established. It was noted that in cases of general negligence whether a person has breached their duty of care is left to the court to determine based on a principle of what was reasonable for a defendant to do in the specific circumstances.

With regard to cases of negligence in healthcare, chapter 5 has discussed how the breach of the duty of care is assessed by reference to the required standard of care and that this standard of care is tested by examining the actions of a healthcare practitioner against the 'Bolam test'.

It was noted that the original 'Bolam test' used in cases alleging negligence in healthcare has been modified since its introduction, although still referred to as the 'Bolam test', and that the test that is currently in use to assess whether the standard of care has been met is:

> whether the healthcare practitioner has acted in accordance with practice accepted as proper by a responsible body of healthcare practitioners who are skilled in the particular aspect of care or treatment, and that this body of opinion can withstand logical and objective scrutiny.

Chapter 5 has highlighted that there are two stages to the 'Bolam test' that a court has to consider when deciding whether the standard of care has been met or whether the healthcare practitioner has breached their duty of care to the patient.

The first stage asks if the practice of the defendant healthcare practitioner is accepted as proper by other healthcare practitioners, and is consistent with what they would do in the same circumstances. The second stage asks if that body of opinion, and thus the practice of the defendant healthcare practitioner, if looked at objectively, has a logical basis to it.

In both general cases of negligence and those involving negligence in healthcare, the determination of whether a defendant has breached their duty of care involves consideration of what was reasonable in the circumstances. In negligence in healthcare, it is the standard of care of the reasonable healthcare practitioner that underpins the decision regarding possible breach of the duty of care.

When determining if a healthcare practitioner has breached their duty of care to a patient, the courts have to base their decision on the evidence supplied to them and their assessment of whether it can withstand logical scrutiny. This results in the application of an external and objective test of the standard of care, which determines whether a defendant acted as a reasonable practitioner would have done in the circumstances. They will, of course, look to previous precedent to assist them in their decision making.

This chapter has suggested that the need to have a logical basis to determine the standard of care in any given set of circumstances has contributed to the development of evidence based practice in healthcare. This is because healthcare practice has to be able to demonstrate that it is based on a reasonable and logical foundation.

With regard to the standard of care for healthcare practitioners, chapter 5 has established that:

5. BREACH OF DUTY AND THE STANDARD OF CARE

- the law requires a minimum standard of care from all healthcare practitioners and failure to meet this minimum standard will result in the healthcare practitioner being said to have breached their duty of care to their patient
- the same standard is applied to all healthcare practitioners and this is tested through use of the 'Bolam test' by comparing their practice to the practice of their peers
- the only difference is that of advanced practitioners, and this is because they are assessed against those healthcare practitioners who formerly undertook those roles. That is, they are not judged against their occupational peer group but practitioners from another occupational peer group
- the 'Bolam test' allows for more than one acceptable way of providing care and treatment. To meet the standard of care, the healthcare practitioner has to prove that the care they provided was reasonable by being acceptable by a reasonable and responsible body of opinion
- a healthcare practitioner does not have to be exceptional to meet the standard, being ordinary is sufficient
- if a healthcare practitioner assumes a duty of care as a Good Samaritan they will have to achieve the standard of care relevant to their ordinary role, unless they act outside of their normal competencies and role
- policies and guidance do not set the standard of care but following policies and guidelines can be used to demonstrate that a healthcare practitioner is practising in accordance with a responsible body of opinion
- there is no team standard of care, each individual healthcare practitioner working within a team will have their own standard of care to achieve
- the standard to be applied in a case of negligence in healthcare is the standard at the time of the alleged

negligence not the standard which applies at the time of the court hearing, which may be some years later
- If a healthcare practitioner can demonstrate that their practice was reasonable accepted practice, this will mean that the claimant cannot prove that the defendant breached the duty of care they were owed, and their case will fail at this point

CHAPTER 6

HARM

This is a relatively short chapter, not because proving harm has occurred is not an important part of a negligence in healthcare claim, it is in fact vital, but because harm is unique because people and their bodies are unique. Two identical negligent actions can result in two very different forms of harm in different individuals. Harm must therefore be judged as a question of fact on a case-by-case basis. The court will decide either that harm has occurred or it has not.

In many cases, whether harm has occurred or not is not an issue, or at least not a complex issue, because it is a matter of fact. If a surgeon cuts the wrong leg off a patient that the leg was cut off is a fact. The issue would be more about the causation of the harm and what damages to pay to the patient. However, these are issues for chapters 7 (causation) and 9 (damages).

One issue with regard to harm is whether the harm that the patient has suffered is a type of harm that can be claimed for in a case of negligence in healthcare.

Therefore, chapter 6 will briefly look at what harm is, what forms of harm are recoverable and, acknowledging that the most severe form of harm that could happen is the death of the patient, this chapter also examines gross negligence manslaughter.

Harm as the third wheel of the milk float

Chapters 4 & 5 discussed the duty of care and the standard that has to be reached to meet that duty respectively. These were noted as being the first and second wheels of the milk float, or the first two elements that need to be proved for a case of negligence in healthcare to succeed.

Once it has been established that a healthcare practitioner owed a duty of care to a patient and breached this duty by not meeting the standard of care required, the next element that needs to be proved is that the patient suffered harm of some form.

This is because negligence is not punitive. It is not a way of punishing a healthcare practitioner for the actions they have taken or their omissions. Therefore, if there is no harm there is nothing to redress and so no negligence in healthcare can have occurred.

It should be noted that, as a general rule of law, a person does not have to take positive action to prevent harm to another person unless an exception to the general rule applies. Exceptions to the general rule are where there is a relationship between the persons, for instance between employers and employees and those in a special relationship. Special relationships were discussed in chapter 4 when examining the duty of care and it was noted that healthcare practitioners and patients are legally considered to have a special relationship.

This is why a healthcare practitioner can be sued for negligence in healthcare by a patient who has suffered harm as a result of the healthcare practitioner's actions and their breach of the duty of care they owe to the patient.

It is the patient who has the burden of proving that they have suffered harm. If either the patient has not suffered harm, or the patient cannot prove the harm was suffered, then the claim for negligence in healthcare will fail at that point.

From a legal perspective, no harm means there has been no negligence. This is because if something untoward happened to a patient, but that patient did not suffer any harm there is nothing that they can claim for as there is nothing that needs to be remedied. You will recall from chapter 3 that the purpose of tort law, including negligence, is to put the person in the position they would have been in had the tort/negligence not occurred. If the patient has not suffered any harm there is no position to revert them to.

Forms of harm

There are various forms of harm that can result as a consequence of negligence in healthcare. Harm, for the purposes of our discission, means any suffering, or physical or psychiatric injury, including death, or any loss, including damage to property, that the patient has experienced.

However, not all forms of harm are recoverable in claims for negligence in healthcare, meaning that it is not possible to claim for them. An example of harm that cannot be recovered is pure economic loss or inconvenience. Pure economic loss is loss without any other harm associated with it. To be able to claim for economic loss there has to be some other form of harm that occurred in addition to the economic loss. Thus, if there is just pure economic loss this is not considered harm in terms of proving a claim for negligence in healthcare. This is because pure economic loss is said to be too remote from a healthcare practitioner's duty of care.

As we will see when damages are explored in chapter 9, the damages that are paid on a successful claim for negligence in healthcare will include a payment relating to any economic loss that the patient has or will suffer.

The harm that is being claimed for does not have to be permanent. If someone were to suffer an injury that they recovered from over time, perhaps after additional treatment, that would still be able to be claimed for.

The following sections deal with specific forms of harm.

Death

If a patient were to die as a result of a negligent act their estate, that is their nominated relatives or friends, would be able to make a claim.

Negligence before birth

To sue someone under a tort, the person who makes the claim has to have a legal personality, this is shorthand for an individual or an organisation which has recognised legal rights and legal obligations.

A child under 18 may be sued, but they will not be held liable for any outcome, for instance the payment of damages, until they are 18. A child under 18 can also sue someone but they need someone over 18 to make the claim on their behalf.

If negligence occurs before a child is born it is the mother who will bring a claim on behalf of the child. However, if the mother herself has not suffered any harm she cannot make the claim on her own behalf as the claim would fail based on there being no harm to her.

An unborn child is not recognised as having a legal personality.

This meant that there was a gap in the law as it was possible for an unborn child to be harmed through the negligent actions of a healthcare practitioner, but no-one could sue because the unborn child does not have a legal personality, and the mother has not suffered any harm herself.

This gap in the law resulted in the Congenital Disabilities (Civil Liabilities) Act 1976. This Act allows a child to sue once they are born for events that happened whilst they were in their mother's womb which resulted in them suffering harm in the form of a disability.

An example of harm would be a healthcare practitioner giving the mother a drug, such as Thalidomide, whilst she is pregnant that causes a disability to form in the child. However, anything that causes the harm to the child is within the remit of the Act and allows the child to make a claim.

The only limitation is that the child cannot sue their own mother for anything she did which caused harm to the child, for instance heavy alcohol drinking, throughout the pregnancy. The child would still need to prove their case according to the usual four criteria of duty of care, breach of that duty, harm and causation.

Physical injury

There are numerous forms of harm that can be classified as physical injury. Examples of harm that have been classed as physical injury over the past years include:

- A surgeon who performed a vasectomy on a patient instead of another operation
- Sustaining a back injury when a patient was being transferred from a bed to a chair in a care home
- A transplant surgeon who removed a healthy kidney instead of the diseased one
- The wrong hip being replaced

- A patient with haemophilia who contracted HIV and hepatitis through a blood transfusion
- Undergoing an allergic reaction on being given a drug the patient was recorded as being allergic to
- A patient suffering irreversible brain damage after receiving the wrong drug during an anaesthetic
- The wrong eye being operated on
- Having permanent mobility issues as a result of damage which occurred as a result of an incorrectly applied leg cast
- A patient who had their vocal cords damaged during throat surgery

As can be seen from this brief list, what counts as physical injury includes actual injury, as well as an illness and acquiring a disability as a result of the healthcare practitioner's actions.

Psychiatric injury

If a patient suffered harm to their mental health they may claim under negligence in healthcare as with a physical injury. To be able to claim for a psychiatric injury the harm has to be one that is medically recognised as a psychiatric injury. That is, it is not just being upset or being distressed. Examples of such injuries include anxiety, depression, and post-traumatic stress disorder. Some psychiatric injuries arise as a consequence of physical injures, such as adjusting to living with a disability or post-traumatic stress disorder. Others arise due to a horrific event, for instance being operated on without adequate pain relief.

Other forms of psychiatric injury can occur without physical injury such as a psychiatric healthcare practitioner misdiagnosing a mental health issue.

There is another aspect to psychiatric injury regarding negligence in healthcare. This is concerned with what are termed

6. HARM

secondary victims. A primary victim is the person to whom harm has occurred, for instance the patient. Whereas a secondary victim is someone that the harm did not occur to but may still be affected by it, for instance the husband of a patient.

A secondary victim may claim that the harm that occurred to their spouse has affected them to the extent that they are now suffering with nervous shock. Nervous shock is the term traditionally used but the more modern term would be post-traumatic stress disorder.

The general legal position is that it is not possible to claim as a secondary victim for nervous shock, although a primary victim can. There are two exceptions to this general rule:

- Where the secondary victim witnessed what happened to the primary victim and it was of a particularly horrifying nature
- Where the secondary victim was told what happened to the primary victim and the way they were told can be said to be negligent. An example would be a husband who is told that their wife has died and given all the graphic and unnecessary details relating to her death

The legal processes by which a secondary victim can make and prove their case is outside the scope of this book. However, in short, the secondary victim has to prove that:

- they have a psychiatric injury that is medically recognised
- this occurred as a result of the 'shock' of seeing or being told about something that was horrifying to them, that happened to someone close to them. Close means someone who whom they have ties of love and affection
- their 'nervous shock' was the result of a single event, if their psychiatric injury progresses over time it would not be seen as harm that can be claimed

- the healthcare practitioner, who they are bringing an action against caused them to suffer the 'nervous shock' though a negligent act or omission
- it is reasonably foreseeable that someone of reasonable constitution would be similarly affected

Pain and suffering

What counts as pain and suffering encompasses quite a wide range of things. It is personalised to the actual patient so what I say is suffering may not seem like suffering to you, and vice versa.

Suffering includes actual pain, suffering in terms of being in a state of anxiety and being fearful. As an example of pain and suffering, let's assume a patient were to wake up from a general anaesthetic whilst undergoing surgery because their anaesthetic was not sufficiently administered, and they were not sufficiently monitored during the operation. They would not receive any actual physical injury and may not be in pain because that part of the anaesthetic was sufficient but would be said to have suffered because of the distress they experienced during the time they were awake.

Loss of chance

This refers to situations where the healthcare practitioner is negligent in making a diagnosis or provides the wrong treatment. The claim would be that as consequence of the negligence the patient has lost the chance of recovering at all or of making a full recovery.

Whilst it is possible to make a claim for loss of chance these claims are extremely difficult and unlikely to succeed because it has to be proved, on the balance of probability, that there is a 51% or higher certainty that the loss of chance has not already occurred. This difficulty is demonstrated in the case of Gregg v Scott [2005].

Mr Gregg went to his general practitioner to have a lump under his left arm assessed. Dr Scott failed to diagnose that Mr Gregg had a form of cancer. It was nine months before the cancer was finally diagnosed, during which time the cancer had spread.

It was determined that had Mr Gregg been diagnosed and received treatment immediately he would have had a 42% chance of a ten year survival. As it was he had a 25% chance of a ten year survival. A ten year survival being the way of calculating a cure.

As Mr Gregg had less than a 50% chance of survival even if he had had immediate treatment, it was judged that he had not had a loss of chance even though the doctor's actions had otherwise been negligent. This is because Mr Gregg could not prove that he had not already lost the chance of a cure at the time he initially went to see his GP, as at that time he only had a 42% chance of a recovery for ten years (the 42% chance of recovery was based on statistical evidence produced during the trial). In other words, it was unlikely that he would have lived for 10 years even if he had been diagnosed and treated immediately, as his chances of this occurring were only 42%.

Wrongful birth

In a claim for wrongful birth the claimant is arguing that because of a negligent act by a healthcare practitioner they have a child that they have to raise, and they are seeking damages to cover the costs of raising the child.

The negligent act by the healthcare practitioner will relate to a vasectomy or sterilisation that has failed in some way.

This was the situation in the McFarlane v Tayside Health Board [1999] case, which concerned a man having a vasectomy to stop having further children and his being told that his vasectomy was successful, and he could dispense with contraception. However, after they stopped using contraception his wife became pregnant and they had a baby daughter.

In the case it was held that *'the parents were not entitled to recover damages for the costs of rearing the child, but the mother was entitled to recover damages for the pain and distress suffered during the pregnancy and in giving birth, and for financial loss associated with the pregnancy'* (McFarlane v Tayside Health Board [1999] at page 961).

Thus, although it is possible to claim for pain and suffering and financial loss relating to an unplanned pregnancy which occurred after negligent advice, a wrongful birth claim will not succeed under negligence in healthcare.

Wrongful life

A claim for wrongful life is an argument that a person should never have been born because they are severely disabled, or their life is highly debilitating in some way.

A wrongful life claim was considered in the case of McKay v Essex Area Health Authority [1982]. In this case a doctor failed to diagnose rubella in a woman in the first few months of her pregnancy. As a consequence, the child was born severely disabled.

The judgment in the case stated that ' a claim for "wrongful life" would be contrary to public policy as a violation of the sanctity of human life' (McKay v Essex Area Health Authority [1982] at page 772).

In chapter 4, when discussing proximity and the duty of care, it was noted that public policy is a reason why a duty of care will be said not to exist. If there is no duty of care owed to a person then no negligence can have occurred.

This means that because of the public policy argument it is not possible to claim negligence in healthcare on the basis of wrongful life, that they should not have been allowed to have been born.

Gross negligence manslaughter

Gross negligence manslaughter is a crime under common law. It can only occur where someone has died.

For a healthcare practitioner to be convicted of gross negligence manslaughter the prosecution would have to prove, beyond a reasonable doubt, that:

- the healthcare practitioner owed a duty of care to the deceased patient
- the healthcare practitioner breached this duty of care through an act or omission which failed to meet the standard of care
- the patient's death was caused by the act or omission of the healthcare practitioner
- the negligence of the healthcare practitioner amounts to gross negligence

Whether a healthcare practitioner was guilty of gross negligence manslaughter was considered in R v Adomako [1994]. In this case an anaesthetist failed to observe that a patient who was anesthetised and being operated on had become disconnected, for a period of six minutes, from the ventilator that was supplying their oxygen. As a consequence of not receiving any oxygen for a prolonged period the patient suffered a cardiac arrest leading to their death.

R v Adomako [1994] has since become a leading case for determining the requirements that have to be met for gross negligence manslaughter to be proved.

Because this is a criminal case involving a charge of manslaughter, it is heard in front of a jury who will find the defendant guilty or not guilty. However, to do so the jury will also have to consider if any negligence has occurred.

Lord MacKay stated that *'the ordinary principles of the law of negligence apply to ascertain whether or not the defendant has been in breach of a duty of care towards the victim who has died. If such breach of duty is established the next question is whether that breach of duty caused the death of the victim. If so, the jury must go on to consider whether that breach of duty should be characterised as gross negligence and therefore as a crime. This will depend on the seriousness of the breach of duty committed by the defendant in all the circumstances in which the defendant was placed when it occurred. The jury will have to consider whether the extent to which the defendant's conduct departed from the proper standard of care incumbent upon him, involving as it must have done a risk of death to the patient, was such that it should be judged criminal'* (R v Adomako [1994] at pages 86–87).

When discussing what amounted to gross negligence it was stated that *'whether the defendant's breach of duty amounted to gross negligence depended on the seriousness of the breach of duty committed by the defendant in all the circumstances in which he was placed when it occurred and whether, having regard to the risk of death involved, the conduct of the defendant was so bad in all the circumstances as to amount in the jury's judgment as to a criminal act or omission'* (R v Adomako [1994] at page 80).

6. HARM

We have included gross negligence manslaughter because as well as the criminal element, there is also a claim that can be made in negligence in healthcare for the death of the patient.

As can be seen, there is overlap between what has to be proved for the crime of gross negligence manslaughter and the civil case of negligence in healthcare. Because criminal cases have priority this would be heard before the civil case.

Summary of chapter 6

Chapter 6 considered the harm aspect of negligence in healthcare.

Various forms of harm have been identified and it was noted that if a patient making a claim in negligence in healthcare cannot prove that they have suffered harm their claim will fail.

The specific instances of secondary victims making a claim for 'nervous shock' and gross negligence manslaughter were explored. Noting that apart from two exceptions it is not possible for a secondary victim to make a claim. That with regard to gross negligence manslaughter there is a criminal element as well as a civil claim.

CHAPTER 7

CAUSATION

Chapter 7 represents the fourth wheel of the milk float which is taking our case of negligence in healthcare forward. The first, second and third wheels did their job of establishing that a duty of care was owed in chapter 4, that the standard of care was breached in chapter 5, and that harm was suffered as discussed in chapter 6.

In this chapter, we discuss how a patient who sues a healthcare practitioner for negligence in healthcare can prove that it was the actions of the healthcare practitioner that did in fact cause the harm that they have suffered.

There are several legal factors that need to be considered before a claimant can be said to have proved that the defendant's action caused them harm. These factors will include 'passing' both a factual test and a legal test and demonstrating that nothing stepped in the way of the healthcare practitioner's actions, and so disrupted the chain of causation.

This chapter will discuss both causation tests and the chain of causation. As well as other legal factors, including the eggshell skull principle.

7. CAUSATION

Proving causation

If a claim for negligence in healthcare has reached this point, the claimant patient will have proved that the defendant healthcare practitioner owed them a duty of care, breached this duty by not meeting the required standard of care, and that this breach of the duty of care caused them harm. However, this is not enough for the claimant to succeed in their claim.

It is not enough because the patient making the claim of negligence in healthcare has to prove that the healthcare practitioner's actions caused the harm they have suffered. It is not enough because it is possible that the patient has suffered harm and the healthcare practitioner breached the duty of care they owed to the patient, but the two are not causally linked. That is the one, the breach of the duty of care, did not cause the other, the harm. In legal terms it would be said that the breach of duty did not cause the harm.

Negligence in healthcare is not established just by proving that something went wrong. There has to be a direct link proved between the action of the healthcare practitioner and the harm. In legal terms this is known as causation, based on the premise that one thing can be shown to cause another.

It is this legal basis of causation that is the focus of this section. There are two legal tests that the patient making a claim has to prove, these can involve a legal doctrine and the absence of any intervening events.

Burden and standard of proof

Before we proceed onto an examination of the legal tests and the legal doctrine, we would remind ourselves that it is the claimant who has the burden of proof in a claim for negligence in healthcare.

The standard of proof is that of the balance of probabilities: that something is more likely to have happened than not.

Proving that the healthcare practitioner's breach of the duty of care they owed to them was the cause of the harm they suffered, is often the greatest challenge the patient acting as a claimant will encounter in making their claim of negligence in healthcare. This is because the law has set a high bar in proving causation. A failure to show a direct causal link between the breach of duty and the harm that resulted is where most claims of negligence in healthcare succeed or fail.

Omission rather than a positive act

In some cases of negligence in healthcare, a patient making a claim is not alleging that it was the actions of the healthcare practitioner which caused the harm they suffered, but rather that the healthcare practitioner did not do something, that they omitted an aspect of care or treatment, that a reasonable body of healthcare practitioners would not have omitted. That it was this omission which directly caused the harm they had suffered.

An omission can be as much a cause of harm in a case of negligence in healthcare as a positive action. Indeed, if we recall the case of Bolitho v City & Hackney Health Authority [1997] from chapter 5, one of the main questions that needed addressing in the case was whether Patrick could have avoided the cardiac arrest which led to his death if he had been intubated on either of the two times he suffered croup earlier in the day.

Therefore, regardless of whether the claimant is alleging that the defendant healthcare practitioner did something or omitted to do something that breached their duty of care to the claimant, the patient acting as a claimant has to prove the same thing: that the breach of the standard of care caused the harm that they suffered.

7. CAUSATION

You may see the distinction between a healthcare practitioner who performs a negligent act and one who makes a negligent omission referred to as the commission and omission argument.

The two tests of causation

Causation as an element in a claim of negligence in healthcare asks a rather simple question: was the harm suffered by the patient caused by the breach of the duty of care and was it reasonably foreseeable?

Although it is a simple question, as noted earlier, it is not that simple to prove. In fact, it requires the claimant to successfully address two separate and distinct aspects of causation to prove their case.

These two aspects of causation are:

- factual causation
- legal causation

Both have to be proved for a claimant to succeed in proving causation and each will be explored in this chapter. However, before we explore them it is time to consider the legal doctrine that has been mentioned, that of *res ipsa loquitur*.

Res ipsa loquitur

Res ipsa loquitur literally means 'the thing speaks for itself' and is a legal doctrine that may be used to establish that the defendant healthcare practitioner was negligent in some, and only some, negligence in healthcare cases, based on the fact that it is possible to infer negligence from the harm that the patient has received.

An example, which was been used previously, is that of a patient who has a healthy kidney removed instead of the diseased one.

The argument based on res ipsa loquitur is that if there was no negligence then the correct kidney would have been removed.

It is sometimes said that if a claimant raises res ipsa loquitur then the burden of proof shifts to the defendant to prove that they were not negligent. This is not actually the case. Rather, it is open to the defendant to put forward an alternative reason as to the cause of the harm rather than negligence on their part.

A commonly used example is that of a surgical scalpel being left inside a patient after an operation. Rather than having to prove causation, the court may allow a claimant to ask the defendant to explain how the scalpel was left inside the patient's body without there being any negligence.

For res ipsa loquitur to succeed for the claimant, the harm must be of a type that cannot happen without there being a negligent act or omission, the defendant is not able to provide an alternative explanation of how the harm was caused that is acceptable to the court, and the defendant has to have had control over what is inferred to be the negligent act or omission.

However, if one of these is missing, for example an alternative reason can be put forward that is acceptable to the court, this removes the application of res ipsa loquitur. Meaning the claimant would still need to satisfy the two tests of causation.

The first test: factual causation

The first test in proving causation is a factual one. It asks whether, as a question of fact, the healthcare practitioner's breach of their duty of care caused the harm the patient suffered.

The way that the factual causation test can be assessed is to ask 'but for'. As in, 'but for' the actions of the defendant would the harm had occurred? If the answer to that question is yes, then

7. CAUSATION

the claimant has not proved causation as there is some other way the harm was caused. However, if the answer to the 'but for' question is no, then the claimant has successfully demonstrated the factual aspect of causation and can move on to proving the legal aspect of causation.

Two cases demonstrate the way in which the courts approach the use of the 'but for' test in cases of negligence in healthcare. The first is a case not related to negligence in healthcare but remains relevant for our purposes.

In Cork v Kirby MacLean Ltd [1952] a man was painting the roof of the defendant's factory at a height of about 20 feet, using a raised platform that did not have guard rails or toe boards. Mr Cork fell from the platform and died.

It was held that there were breaches of the relevant safety regulations regarding the lack of safety equipment. Thus, the defendants could have been held liable because of the breach of safety regulations and thus negligent in respect of Mr Cork's death.

However, the issue of causation was made difficult because Mr Cork had epilepsy and did not inform Kirby MacLean Ltd of this fact. Mr Cork had only been working for Kirby MacLean Ltd for two days but had been treated for epilepsy for several years and he was aware that he could have an epileptic fit at any time, and had expressly been told by his doctor not to work at heights.

In fact, Mr Cork had suffered an epileptic fit which had caused him to fall from the platform. Therefore, Kirby MacLean Ltd argued that they were not liable for Mr Cork's death as it was attributable to his epilepsy of which they were unaware.

Lord Denning stated that *'if you can say that the damage would not have happened but for a particular fault, then that fault is in fact a cause of the damage; but if you can say that the damage would have happened just the same, fault or no fault, then the fault is not a cause of the damage'* (Cork v Kirby MacLean Ltd [1952] at page 407).

Lord Denning then went on to discuss two possible causes of Mr Cork's death, that of Mr Cork in not telling his employers about his epilepsy and his doctor's instruction not to work at height, and the lack of safety provision by Kirby MacLean Ltd.

He noted that Mr Cork's fault in not informing his employer of his epilepsy, and working at a height was a cause of his death. However, Lord Denning also noted that *'a guard-rail and toe-boards might have saved him from falling.. it probably would have saved him. On that view the employers' fault was also one of the causes of the man's death'* (Cork v Kirby MacLean Ltd [1952] at page 407).

Lord Denning was of the opinion that 'but for' the lack of guard-rails or toe-boards Mr Cork would not have died. Although he also believed that 'but for' Mr Cork failing to inform his employers of his epilepsy and ignoring the instruction to work at height he would not have died. He therefore found them equally to blame and awarded damages to be split 50:50 between the two parties. What this means is that the employer, Kirby MacLean Ltd, only have to pay 50% of what the total damages were calculated as being. The other 50% is paid by the claimant, the estate of Mr Cork. As Mr Cork's estate would in effect be paying themselves, in reality it means that the claimant only receives the proportion of the damages that is attributable to the defendants. The other 50% of the damages are lost.

The second case is that of Barnett v Chelsea & Kensington Hospital Management Committee [1968]. The facts of the case were outlined in chapter 4 when discussing to whom a duty of care is owed to. In brief, three night watchmen had drunk tea

7. CAUSATION

and started vomiting shortly afterwards. They all walked to the casualty department but were not seen by the casualty officer who told them via a nurse to see their general practitioners.

Mr Barnett, one of the three night watchmen, died a few hours later from arsenic poisoning.

It was stated in chapter 4 that the judge in the case, Justice Nield, had held that there was a duty of care owed by the casualty officer, Dr Banerjee, to Mr Barnett. Further, Justice Nield held that '*without doubt Dr Banerjee should have seen and examined the deceased*' (Barnett v Chelsea & Kensington Hospital Management Committee [1968] at page 1073).

Thus, the duty of care, breach of that duty, and harm had been proved. The issue that was left to prove was that of causation. Using the 'but for' test, the question that needed answering was, but for the actions of Dr Banerjee would Mr Barnett have died?

It was decided that regardless of any action by Dr Banerjee, Mr Barnett would have died anyway. This was because once a fatal quantity of arsenic has been ingested then no treatment would have saved the patient's life.

Although Dr Banerjee breached his duty of care to Mr Barnett and Mr Barnett suffered harm, there was no factual causation between the breach of the duty of care and the harm suffered. The harm would have occurred regardless. Therefore, there was no negligence.

Material contribution to the harm

Proving that the breach of their duty of care by the healthcare practitioner caused the harm that the patient suffered can be very difficult. This is especially so where there can be more than one cause of the harm.

The Wilsher v Essex Area Health Authority [1986] case has been discussed previously in both chapters 4 & 5, with the facts of the case outlined in chapter 4 in the decision on team liability. The case is important in causation as well, because in the case it was stated that a claimant can prove causation by either proving that the breach caused the harm, or that the breach materially contributed to the harm. Thus, the actions of a defendant do not have to be the sole cause of the harm for them to be held liable.

Thus, although there may be more than one factor that could have resulted in the harm that occurred, if the patient making a claim of negligence in healthcare by a healthcare practitioner can prove that the healthcare practitioner directly caused the harm or that their actions were such that they contributed to or increased the risk of harm, factual causation will be satisfied.

Intervening acts

An intervening act is one that breaks the chain of events. The legal phrase is n*ovus actus interveniens* which can be translated as a new act intervenes. What breaking the chain of causation means is that an event has happened but instead of that leading directly to outcome X, another event occurs, the intervening act, which affects the outcome, so that now outcome Y occurs.

This means that although a healthcare practitioner breached their duty of care to a patient and this breach set in motion a chain of events which would have led to the patient suffering harm, something else intervened, and that intervening act is said to be the cause of the harm that results.

The intervening act could be a new act by the healthcare practitioner, an act by the patient, or an act by a third party.

An intervening act breaking the chain of causation occurred in the case of McKew v Holland & Hannen & Cubitts (Scotland)

Ltd. [1969]. In that case a man was injured during his employment and as a consequence his leg sometimes gave way. Initially it was said that he would have recovered from this in a couple of weeks, and his employers were found to be liable. However, subsequently the man was going down a steep set of stairs without a handrail when his leg again gave way and he collapsed, resulting in him breaking his ankle.

The question for the court was whether the employers were liable for the fractured ankle as a direct consequence of the original liability. It was held that they were not because the man acted unreasonably by walking down a steep set of stairs without any form of support either from a handrail or another person, and therefore his actions broke the chain of causation from the original injury.

The second test: legal causation

The second test that a claimant has to meet to prove causation is that of legal causation. This requires the claimant to establish that the harm they suffered was a reasonably foreseeable consequence of the healthcare practitioner's actions. In legal terms this is known as establishing that the harm was not too remote from the negligent act.

Whether the harm is too remote or not is a matter for the court to decide in each case.

The rule of remoteness as an aspect of proving causation was established in the case of Overseas Tankship (U.K.) Ltd v Morts Dock and Engineering Co Ltd [1961]. This was a non-healthcare related case. It concerned a spillage of oil from a ship spilling into a bay and subsequently causing damage to a wharf due to a fire caused by a spark from a workshop on the wharf. The question the court had to answer was whether the damage to the wharf was caused by the negligent discharge of oil from the ship.

It was held that the damage to the wharf caused by the fire was too remote from the negligent act 'as a reasonable man would not, on the facts of this case, have foreseen such injury' (Overseas Tankship (U.K.) Ltd v Morts Dock and Engineering Co Ltd [1961] at page 404).

In this way, remoteness as a way of proving legal causation is related to the need to establish proximity for a duty of care to exist, as discussed in chapter 4 when the requirements set by the Caparo Industries plc v Dickman and others [1990] were raised, where it was first stated as a requirement in proving negligence.

There is a link between a defendant not being held liable for harm that a reasonable person would not foresee as resulting from a breach of duty, and the fact that causation will not be established if the harm is too remote from the breach of duty. In either case, where the harm that results is not one that can be reasonably foreseen, a defendant will not be held liable for it.

The claimant does not need to prove that the exact harm they suffered was a reasonably foreseeable consequence of the healthcare practitioner's actions. Rather, they have to prove that the type of harm they suffered would have been reasonably foreseeable by a responsible healthcare practitioner as a consequence of the breach of the duty of care owed to them.

Novus actus interveniens revisited

Essentially when a *novus actus interveniens* occurs, the harm that ultimately happens is said to be too remote from an initial breach of the duty of care to impose a liability on the healthcare practitioner who committed the initial breach.

7. CAUSATION

Eggshell skull rule

The eggshell skull rule is also known as the 'thin skull' rule.

The eggshell skull rule is a legal rule that is used when a defendant may try to argue that the harm that was caused to the patient is too remote to impose a liability on them because they could not have foreseen that this patient had a particular characteristic about them that resulted in the harm.

What the eggshell skull rule effectively says is that you must take the person as you find them. That it is not the person's fault that they have a thin skull and so it is not a defence to causation to argue that a normal person without the characteristic of the defendant would either not have suffered the harm or would have suffered a lesser harm.

For instance, a person with a normal skull may not be harmed when struck by a soft ball at a slow speed, however a person with a very thin or a fragile skull, the so-called eggshell skull, may be harmed by a soft ball thrown at a slow speed that hits them on the head. In such a situation the defendant's argument would be that no-one can know the person has an eggshell skull, and so they couldn't have foreseen that the harm would occur if it wouldn't occur in most people. In such a situation the defendant's argument would be that no-one can know the person has an eggshell skull, and so they couldn't have foreseen that the harm would occur if it wouldn't occur in most people. However, such an argument would fail under the eggshell skull rule.

Summary of chapter 7

Causation is the 4th wheel of the milk float. If a claimant can prove that a healthcare practitioner's actions caused the harm that they suffered, this will allow their case, and the milk float, to proceed. Further consideration could then be given to whether there are any other defences that the healthcare practitioner can argue removes their liability in relation to the negligence in healthcare claim by the patient.

Sometimes it is possible to infer negligence from the harm that the patient has received and the doctrine of *res ipsa loquitur* can be used to establish causation.

However, in most cases, the assessment of whether causation has been proved or not is based on two separate tests: the factual test and the legal test. The burden of proving causation is on the claimant and is judged using the balance of probabilities.

Factual causation is based on the claimant proving that 'but for' the actions of the healthcare practitioner the harm would not have occurred.

Legal causation is based on the remoteness of the harm that occurred. Although a claimant may have proved that the defendant factually caused their harm by use of the 'but for' test, it may still be possible for causation not to be proved if the claimant cannot demonstrate that the harm they suffered was reasonably foreseeable as a consequence of the healthcare practitioner's breach of the duty owed to them.

If causation cannot be proved by the claimant, then the defendant will not be held liable for any harm.

CHAPTER 8

DEFENCES

There are several defences that are available to a defendant who is defending their practice in a case involving negligence in healthcare. Therefore, the focus of chapter 8 is on the ways that a healthcare practitioner may defend a claim of negligence in healthcare made against them.

Defences in legal cases

Any legal case will have two opposing sides, each trying to prove that they are right, and the other side is wrong. Even if the side bringing the case, in civil cases that is the claimant, can prove the facts of their case and have the law correctly applied, it is possible for them not to be successful because the defendant has raised a defence that is held to be valid.

Whilst this may seem to be unfair or unjust, the law requires that for a party to successful argue their case they need to establish the facts, apply the law to those facts and for there to be a lack of a valid defence by the defendant. If any of these three criteria, the facts, application of the law, and lack of a valid defence, cannot be established by the claimant the case will not be proved.

If we return to our milk float analogy, if a defendant is able to raise a valid defence they have in effect applied the brake to stop the milk float from moving forward.

The defences that are discussed in this chapter are ones that it is possible for a defendant to raise in a case involving negligence in healthcare. However, that does not mean that in all cases of negligence in healthcare a patient making the claim has to prove all the four elements of negligence and then go on to prove that the defendant's defence is not valid. In most cases of negligence in healthcare cases a defence is not raised. Rather the dispute is centred on the four elements of negligence.

Defences available in cases of negligence in healthcare

There are several defences that will be discussed in this chapter. Some of these defences have been discussed in the preceding chapters, either specifically noted as being a defence to negligence in healthcare, or as part of a general discussion relating to the subject matter of the specific chapter. We have raised them again for the sake of completeness, so that the possibility of using them as a defence can be put into context with the other defences available to a defendant.

The defences that are said to be available to a healthcare practitioner defending themselves against an allegation of negligence in healthcare are:

- Mistaken identity
- Dispute over the facts
- One of the four elements of negligence has not been proved
- Novus actus interveniens
- Contributory negligence
- Volenti non fit injuria
- Statutory limitation

In the sections that follow, each of these will be explored.

8. DEFENCES

Mistaken identity

If a patient were to make a claim for negligence in healthcare against Andy but Andy did not actually care for or treat the patient at all, because it was Marc who treated the patient, Andy could raise the defence of mistaken identity.

If it was Marc and not Andy that treated the patient it would be unfair for Andy to be the one who is found to have been negligent. However, whilst this is a theoretical defence available in negligence cases, it is very very unlikely to be one that is used in a case involving negligence in healthcare.

It would be rare that a patient did not know the healthcare practitioner who was caring for them or treating them. Further, it is a part of the pre-trial aspect of a negligence in healthcare case to establish who the healthcare practitioners involved in the patient's care and treatment were. So that the actual sequence of events can be determined to see if there is a non-broken chain of causation from the actions of one or more of the healthcare practitioners to the harm that the patient suffered.

Finally, even if the actual healthcare practitioner could not be identified, which would be rare, it would be the employing healthcare organisation that would actually be sued.

We have included discussion of mistaken identity because we have erroneously seen it raised in discussion of negligence in healthcare, and to note that the use of mistaken identity as a defence applies in criminal cases. It is not a defence that can be expected to be raised in a case of negligence in healthcare.

Dispute over the facts

This is another example of a defence, as with mistaken identity, that is not really a defence.

It should be noted though that, unlike mistaken identity, a dispute over the facts could mean that the patient's case is not successful. However, this is not because a dispute over the facts has been raised as a defence but rather that on the balance of probabilities it is decided that the defendant's version of events, the facts, are more likely than not to have occurred than the claimant's.

There are two questions that a patient would have to prove to be successful in a claim for negligence in healthcare, the question of fact and the question of law. As noted in chapter 5, a question of fact is about whether an event happened or whether something met the required level. Whereas a question of law is about applying the law to those facts and asking what legal remedy is available to correct the wrong where one has occurred.

If the patient is not able to establish that their version of events is what happened then they will be unable to prove negligence in healthcare occurred.

The wheels have come off the milk float

Throughout this book we have used the analogy of a milk float as a way of discussing aspects of negligence in healthcare. One point we have made is that the milk float needs four wheels to keep moving forward and thus if one of the wheels comes off the milk float stops.

In a similar way if a patient is unable to prove one of the four elements of negligence in healthcare their claim will stop at that point. This is because to establish that negligence in healthcare has occurred all four elements have to be proved, it is not enough for only two or three of the elements to be proved if one or more is not proved.

8. DEFENCES

Thus, the patient making a claim of negligence in healthcare against a healthcare practitioner has to prove that the healthcare practitioner owed them a duty of care (as discussed in chapter 4), that this duty of care was breached by a failure to meet the required standard (as discussed in chapter 5), that they suffered harm (as discussed in chapter 6), and that it was the breach of the duty of care by the healthcare practitioner that caused the harm they suffered (as discussed in chapter 7).

It is on the balance of probabilities that a patient has to prove their case. There are two possible ways in which the wheels may come off the milk float. The first is that the patient is not able to establish one of the four elements of negligence in healthcare at all, for instance that they suffered harm. The second is that the patient is unable to prove one or more of the elements on the balance of probabilities, for instance that the harm they suffered was caused by the healthcare practitioner's breach of the duty of care owed to them.

A failure to prove one of the four elements of negligence in healthcare by the claimant is not really a defence that is raised by the defendant. Rather it can be seen as an aspect of the adversarial nature of civil cases in the courts of the United Kingdom, one side will prove their case and one side won't.

A patient will not succeed in their claim for negligence in healthcare if:

- they were not owed a duty of care by the defendant
- the defendant did not breach their duty of care. For example, if a healthcare practitioner can prove that they satisfied the requirements of the 'Bolam test', as discussed in chapter 5, they will stop the patient's case progressing any further
- the patient did not suffer harm

175

- the breach of the duty of care by the healthcare practitioner did not cause the harm the patient suffered

It is probably true to say that where a patient is unable to prove their case of negligence in healthcare against a healthcare practitioner, it is the failure to demonstrate a causal link between the harm they have suffered and the actions of the healthcare practitioner where the majority of cases of negligence in healthcare succeed or breakdown. This is because it can be very hard to separate the various factors that contribute to an event and categorically prove that a particular action by a healthcare practitioner was the cause of the harm suffered.

Novus actus interveniens

Again, this is not a true defence as such, but rather an argument that would be put forward challenging the element of causation. It has been discussed previously in chapter 7, but we raise it again to note that even if a healthcare practitioner breached the duty of care to a patient and the patient suffered harm, it may still be possible for the healthcare practitioner not to be held liable if an intervening act were to be held to break the chain of causation.

As explained in chapter 7, an intervening act is said to make the harm that ultimately happens too remote from the initial breach of the duty of care to pose a liability on the healthcare practitioner who committed that initial breach. Thus, although it is not a separate defence, it can result in a wheel coming off the milk float in the same way as discussed in the previous section.

Contributory negligence

Contributory negligence occurs where the patient making the claim of negligence in healthcare is said to have contributed to the harm they have suffered.

8. DEFENCES

It is a defence that can be raised by the defendant but is known as a partial defence. This is because it does not absolve the healthcare practitioner of liability in total but rather will apportion blame to both the healthcare practitioner and the patient.

In contributory negligence, the healthcare practitioner will still have breached their duty of care to the patient resulting in harm to the patient caused by that breach, but the patient will have materially contributed to the harm they have suffered. Therefore, the healthcare practitioner is still found to be negligent.

The effect of a patient being found to have contributed to their own harm is in relation to damages. Damages will be discussed primarily in chapter 9 but here we will just say that, if a patient were held to have contributed to their own harm, the amount of damages they would otherwise receive will be reduced by a sum proportionate to their contribution to the overall negligence.

So rather than not being successful in their case of negligence in healthcare because they contributed to the harm they suffered, the patient can still prove their case but the fact that they contributed to their own harm will be recognised through a reduction in damages.

This is laid down in the Law Reform (Contributory Negligence) Act 1945. Section 1(10) of this Act states that:

'Where any person suffers damage as the result partly of his own fault and partly of the fault of any other person or persons, a claim in respect of that damage shall not be defeated by reason of the fault of the person suffering the damage, but the damages recoverable in respect thereof shall be reduced to such extent as the court thinks just and equitable having regard to the claimant's share in the responsibility for the damage'.

It is a matter for the court to calculate the proportion of the patient's contribution to the harm they suffered. The court can then reduce the amount of damages the patient would receive by a similar proportion.

The ways that a patient could materially contribute to their own harm can include anything where the patient does not take responsibility for their own safety, for example:

- not following post operative instructions
- failing to notify a healthcare practitioner of an allergy or a previous illness that is relevant to the care and treatment they are receiving
- not taking medication as prescribed
- not attending follow-up consultations

Contributory negligence was discussed in chapter 7 in relation to the case of Cork v Kirby MacLean Ltd [1952]. In that case it was held that Mr Cork was equally to blame for the accident that occurred, and thus contributed to his own death, and the damages that would otherwise have been awarded were reduced by 50%.

A child can be held to be contributory negligent but when this is being assessed it should be judged against the standard of someone of their own age.

Volenti non fit injuria

Volenti non fit injuria can be translated from the Latin as 'to a willing person, it is not a wrong'. It is a legal principle used as a defence in negligence cases where a person voluntarily agrees to a risk of harm which subsequently materialises.

The reason that it can be used as a defence is because the purpose of tort law is to right a wrong. If a person has voluntarily assumed a risk of harm, the principle means that they cannot sue for that harm due to their voluntary assumption of the risk that resulted in the harm.

8. DEFENCES

By assuming a risk, a person is absolving another person of any consequences related to that risk. It is a way of stopping a claimant "having their cake and eating it".

If the defence is used it would be a complete defence where it can be shown that the claimant voluntarily agreed to the risk that resulted in any consequent harm. Although in using the defence successfully it has to be shown that the person assuming the risk is fully aware of all the risks and had free choice to assume the risk or not, and was aware of the actual harm that could result.

However, volenti non fit injuria is rarely used in negligence in healthcare cases.

It needs to be pointed out that the principle of volenti non fit injuria is not the same as a patient providing their consent for a treatment or operation. Consent is a defence to the torts of battery and trespass to the person (which are discussed in chapter 3) but not to negligence in healthcare.

Statutory limitation

There are prescribed statutory periods within which a claim has to be started. If the claim is not started within the prescribed statutory time, it is a defence for the defendant to raise this fact. If it is successfully raised it would be a complete defence and the claim would be said to be statutorily barred from proceeding.

The statutory limitation periods are contained within the Limitation Act 1980. Section 2 states that *'an action founded on tort shall not be brought after the expiration of six years from the date on which the cause of action accrued'*. Thus, any claim for harm resulting from any tort is statutorily barred after six years.

With regard to negligence, the relevant period is found in section 11 (2) which states that: *the period applicable is three years from*

(a) the date on which the cause of action accrued; or
(b) the date of knowledge (if later) of the person injured'

This means that a claim for negligence in healthcare has to be started within three years of the date of the negligent act, or three years from when the patient was aware that they suffered harm as a result of a negligent act, or when they should have been aware judged by when a reasonable person would have been aware.

Although if the patient dies then according to section 11(5) the period is '*three years from*

(a) the date of death; or
(b) the date of the personal representative's knowledge;whichever is the later'

There are two exceptions to these rules regarding limitation periods. The first is in relation to children, where the three-year limitation period starts from the child's 18th birthday, so they have until they are 21 to commence a claim. The second is in relation to a patient who does not have mental capacity, in which case there is no limitation period to commence a claim. Although if the patient subsequently regains their mental capacity the three-year period begins.

Section 33 of the Limitation Act 1980 does allow the courts some discretion to allow a claim to proceed even if it is outside of the limitation period where it is in the interests of justice to do so. However, this is a discretion and so it would be unwise to rely on this to delay commencing a claim.

It is important to note that the limitation period relates to the commencement of a claim, not the time within which a claim has to be heard in court and settled. By commencement of a

8. DEFENCES

claim, we mean the issuing of a claim form, sometimes known as issuing court proceedings against the defendant.

The reason for having a limitation period is twofold. Firstly, because the longer the period from an event to an actual hearing, the harder it may be for a claimant to prove their case. Because the recollection of individuals involved may become poor and thus unreliable, and health records could be lost with the passage of time. Secondly, to protect potential defendants from having claims made many years after an event.

A failure to commence a claim for negligence in healthcare within the statutory limitation period is a major reason why patients do not succeed in their claims against healthcare practitioners.

Summary of chapter 8

In a claim for negligence in healthcare it is only after the four elements of negligence have been proved, that is that the four wheels of the milk float have been shown to turn smoothly, and the defendant is not able to raise a valid defence, or apply the brake on the milk float, that the court can impose liability and award damages.

There are many defences available to defendants in civil legal cases. Although theoretically available to defendants in negligence in healthcare cases, many of these are not true defences.

The two main defences that are used in negligence in healthcare cases are contributory negligence by the patient and the claim by the patient being outside the statutory limitation period.

A defence of contributory negligence is only a partial defence and in effect will reduce the damages payable by the defendant by the proportion of the negligence that is attributable to the patient: the part they contributed to the harm.

Whereas a defence that the claim is outside the statutory limitation period is a complete defence and, if upheld, results in the claim failing.

CHAPTER 9

DAMAGES

This chapter is concerned with the award that is made at the end of a successful claim of negligence in healthcare by a patient. It begins by examining what damages are and what the purpose of them is. It then proceeds to look at the award of damages, including how damages are paid and the types of damages that are payable.

Following this there is an examination of how damages are calculated. Finally, we discuss what may reduce the amount of damages paid.

What are damages?

As was noted in chapter 3, negligence in healthcare is a tort, this means that the case that has been brought by a patient is to seek redress for a wrong that has been committed to them. Also noted in chapter 3 is that the legal remedy for a tort is a monetary award, that is damages. The purpose of which is to put the claimant back in the position they would have been in had the wrong not occurred. In law this is known by the Latin phrase 'restitutio in integrum', which translates as restitution to the original.

Not all cases of negligence in healthcare will result in an award of damages. It is only when the four elements of negligence in healthcare have been proved, as discussed in chapters 4 through

8, that the patient can be said to be successful in their claim and damages will be awarded.

As stated above, damages are the only remedy that is available in claims under tort law, thus all a patient who is successful in a case of negligence in healthcare against a healthcare practitioner can expect to receive is a monetary award. Nothing else. There is no expectation of an apology or a reason as to why the harm happened, just the monetary award.

In chapter 3 when examining the purpose of negligence in healthcare it was noted that it is not as easy to put a person who has suffered negligence in healthcare back in the position they would have been in were it not for the negligent act, as it is with other forms of negligence. The example given in chapter 3 was that of negligence in repairing the milk float, when an award of damages can be used to pay for the necessary repairs to return the milk float to as it was before the harm occurred to it.

As it may not be possible to restore the patient to the position they were in prior to them suffering the harm which occurred as a result of the healthcare practitioner's breach of the duty of care owed to them, the damages will need to be carefully calculated. This is because the damages awarded need to include anything and everything that is necessary to restore the patient to their position before the harm happened and to pay for any adjustments that are needed where full restoration is not possible, and to compensate the patient for the fact that the harm occurred.

The calculation of damages and the types of damages payable is explored further in this chapter.

Terminology of damages

There can be some confusion over the terms used when discussing damages, as some terms are very similar to each

9. DAMAGES

other and for others different words are used for the same thing.

The following are some of the more common terms and the way that we would use them.

Damages – a sum of money awarded at the end of a successful claim of negligence in healthcare that is designed to put, or attempt to put, the patient in the position they would have been in had the harm not occurred.

Damage – another term for the harm that is suffered as a result of the negligence in healthcare. Not to be confused with damages. Damage is the harm suffered and damages is the monetary award in respect of that harm.

Harm – means any suffering, or physical or psychiatric injury, including death, or any loss, including damage to property, that the patient has experienced.

Loss – another term for the harm suffered. Specifically used in relation to a sum of money that is not received, for instance wages when the patient is unable to work, or in relation to future income that will not be received as in 'future loss of income'.

Quantum – an assessment of the value of the harm suffered. Another way of saying damages.

Compensation – this is another term for damages. However, sometimes this is referred to as a specific part of an award of damages. This usually occurs to differentiate between two aspects of damages. When this happens, it is said that damages is the money to right the wrong, and compensation is paid as a way of acknowledging, or making amends for, the fact that the wrong happened in the first place.

In fact, as we will soon see, any award of money made will be intended to cover the acknowledgment of the wrong and the money to right the wrong, as far as it is possible to do so.

The award of damages

At the end of a successful claim of negligence in healthcare the patient making the claim will be awarded damages. As has been discussed earlier in this chapter, the damages are a sum of money awarded to compensate the patient for the fact that a wrong was committed, the negligent act, and for the harm they suffered, and indeed may still be suffering, and to try, as far as is possible, to put the patient back in the position they were in before the negligent act.

The total sum of damages awarded will reflect the harm that the patient has suffered. Therefore, the greater the harm the higher the award of damages will be. Although the negligent act that caused the harm, the breach of the duty of care by the healthcare practitioner, reflects unlawful conduct, damages are not awarded as a punishment for the healthcare practitioner.

We feel that it is important to state that the award of damages is not a punishment, because it can come across as a punishment when reading and listening to reports of the awards made in cases of negligence in healthcare. So, to reiterate, the award of damages is made solely to put the patient back in the position they were in before the negligent act, as far as it is possible to do so.

Now, having said that the award of damages is not a punishment, we have to recognise that punitive damages, that is damages that are given as a punishment, can be awarded in the United Kingdom but that is very rare in cases of negligence in healthcare.

Punitive damages, also known as aggravated damages or more commonly exemplary damages, can be awarded if the court believes that they are necessary to act as a deterrent for the defendant or other healthcare practitioners from committing

9. DAMAGES

the same negligent act. They can also be awarded where the defendant healthcare practitioner's breach of the duty of care was so appalling that it needs to be recognised separately, to acknowledge the effect healthcare practitioner's misconduct has had on the patient over and above that of the harm itself. It is possible that an extreme example of negligence in healthcare may attract an award of punitive damages.

However, punitive damages are rarely awarded in cases of negligence in healthcare,

They are more likely to be awarded in a case where a claimant was injured by a driver who was drunk, to recognise that the driver was grossly negligent.

If punitive damages were to be awarded, they will be awarded additionally and announced separately to the normal award of damages. This is in recognition that where an award of punitive damages is made, it is this that acts as the 'punishment' or 'deterrent', not the normal award of damages.

How is the award of damages made?

The next section discusses the specifics of what is included in the award of damages. However, the award of damages is a final award, by which we mean that it is not generally possible to go back to the court and ask for more money. For this reason, the amount of damages awarded has to be carefully calculated to take account of all the present and future needs of the patient.

The traditional and currently the most frequent way of paying damages is through a one-off lump sum payment. Sometimes referred to as a once and for all payment. Whilst this may be welcomed by the patient who has succeeded in their claim it can be problematic.

The benefits of a one-off lump sum payment are:

- it gives finality to the claim. The claim has succeeded, and the damages have been received. The claim is thus over
- the patient who has received the award of damages has control and flexibility as to how they use the money. They can invest it to provide for their future care needs if they have any or choose to do something else with it

The disadvantages of a one-off lump sum payment are:

- with a large award of damages, the patient may have to pay for financial advice on how to manage their money
- if the patient is severely injured as a result of the harm they suffered, their future care needs may increase in cost and the amount of damages awarded may run out
- any money that is invested is subject to taxes

In recognition of the disadvantages of a one-off lump sum payment, in 1989 structured settlements were introduced. These have since become known as periodical payments. Initially if a periodical payment was to be used for the payment of damages it had to be agreed by both the claimant and the defendant. Now it is possible for the court to impose a Periodical Payment Order.

A Periodical Payment Order is normally only made by the court in cases where the patient has suffered severe injuries, and it would be difficult to calculate the future care costs, or for an award of damages to a child. The court has to consider that it is in the best interests of the patient to impose a Periodical Payment Order before it can be made. Although one can be agreed between the claimant and defendant.

The effect of a Periodical Payment Order on the award of damages is that the patient would receive an annual payment for the rest of their life. The amount of the annual payment can be varied, subject to provision within the original award of damages and to reflect changes in inflation and other factors.

9. DAMAGES

As well as the annual payment, when the damages are paid via a Periodical Payment Order, there is usually a one-off payment also made. This payment is to allow any immediate care needs to be addressed and, as an example, any adaptations that need to be made to the patient's house to be undertaken. The lump sum payment also incorporates the sum of money awarded to compensate the patient for the fact that a wrong was committed.

The annual payment made under a Periodical Payment Order is made for the life of the patient.

The advantages of a Periodical Payment Order are:

- the patient does not have to worry about the damages running out
- the patient knows that they have a regular payment and that this will increase in line with inflation, allowing them to manage their resources more effectively
- if the patient's needs change this can be reflected in a variation to the Periodical Payment Order
- a payment received via a Periodical Payment Order is not taxable, neither are they considered in relation to assessment of means-tested state benefits

There are disadvantages with a Periodical Payment Order, these include:

- they do not allow the patient's experience and claim to be finalised as there are ongoing payments being received
- if the patient dies prematurely the payments will cease as they are only for the life of the patient. This could affect their dependants
- if the patient's condition improves it is possible that the annual payment is varied downward

Periodical Payment Orders are not usually used where the total amount of damages awarded is less than £1 million. Indeed, one-off lump sum payments still remain the most common way of awarding damages in cases of negligence in healthcare.

Heads of damages

We appreciate that this may seem to be a rather weird title for a section. Heads of damage is the term used to refer to the totality of the various categories of damage or loss that will be paid as part of the overall award of damages. Head means type or category; therefore, a head of damage refers to a specific identifiable category of damage.

Heads of damages refer to the categories when they are part of an overall award, whereas heads of claim refer to the categories that the claimant is seeking as part of their claim.

It has been acknowledged that the award of damages is a final once and for all payment, although it is possible for payments to be made on a regular basis as discussed in the previous section. The point is that an award of damages should be seen as the legal mechanism whereby a patient, who has suffered harm as a consequence of the negligent actions of a healthcare practitioner, is provided with the means, in the form of financial resources, to restore them to the position they were in prior to the harm occurring.

Recognising that it is not always possible to put the patient back in the position they would have been in had the harm not occurred, that is a full restoration, the award of damages has to ensure that any future needs are provided for.

Therefore, when the court is considering the award of damages, there are lots of heads of claim that need to be considered to ensure that the award fully acknowledges the harm occurred and mitigates against the consequences of the harm the patient has suffered, including the patient's past losses and their future needs.

The rest of this section will outline the various heads of damages that may be included in an award of damages to a patient who has suffered harm as a result of negligence in healthcare by a healthcare practitioner.

Special and general damages

An award of damages is calculated in two main categories, those heads of damage that fall under special damages and those that fall under general damages.

Special damages are financial losses that can be accurately calculated. Whereas general damages are those losses that cannot be accurately calculated.

Lawyers and the courts tend to refer to pecuniary and non-pecuniary losses, with pecuniary losses being financial losses, and non-pecuniary referring to anything that is not a financial loss. So special damages would be for pecuniary losses and general damages awarded for non-pecuniary losses and harm.

Another way of considering the difference between special and general damages is that special damages can be quantified, and general damages are non-quantifiable.

Specific heads of damages

The following are examples of specific heads of damages that may be awarded as part of an overall award of damages. The heads of damages are the same irrespective of where the patient is an adult or a child, but the amount awarded would take this into consideration.

We have separated the heads of damages into those that would be classified as special damages and those as general damages.

Special damages:

- loss of income to date of trial as a result of the harm suffered. Usually refers to loss of wages
- loss of earning capacity, refers to loss of future wages as a result of not being able to work or having to take a lower paid job
- care costs, meaning the cost of having to have care provided when the patient is unable to do something that they used to do for themselves. Includes both care costs incurred to the date of trial and future care costs. For a child where the care is provided by a parent, this could include the parent's loss of earnings
- healthcare costs, both those already incurred and those for future treatment needs. Includes the cost of paying for private medical care and treatment and all associated costs, such as diagnostic tests and investigations, medications, physiotherapy, and any surgery, in-patient hospital stays and out-patient consultations. With reference to future medical care and treatment, the fact that this may be available on the NHS is ignored and it is the cost of providing this privately that is used
- interest, this is not a loss as such but a sum award for the delay in receiving the award of special damages from the date that the harm occurred
- loss of services, this refers to the fact that a patient who has suffered harm may no longer be able to manage the normal household activities that they were used to doing such as gardening, general house maintenance, cleaning etc and the cost of having to have these provided
- aids and appliances that are needed to enable the patient to live their life as fully as possible, for instance prosthetic limbs or a wheelchair
- pension loss, where the patient is unable to work and so

9. DAMAGES

is not able to pay into an occupational pension scheme
- costs of bringing the claim, including legal fees
- accommodation, the cost of having to purchase and move to another house suitable for the patient's disabilities, or the costs of making adaptations and renovations to the patient's home
- vehicle costs such as, the cost of a replacement adaptive vehicle or the cost of making appropriate adaptations to the patient's current vehicle
- transportation costs incurred to travelling to healthcare appointments
- out-of-pocket expenses, money that the patient would not have spent had it not been for the harm they suffered
- balancing payment, this reflects the fact that the award of damages is paid as a lump sum based on today's values, and that the patient will need to invest it to pay for future care needs etc.. Althugh an award of damages is not taxable, any interest earned is taxable and so the balancing payment takes into account any loss of income that the patient could expect to receive from their award of damages, so that the patient is not disadvantaged

General damages:

- pain, suffering and loss of amenity. Loss of amenity is also known as loss of enjoyment of life. This can include the physical, psychological and emotional impairment and impact of the harm mental pain and anguish. It is a payment in recognition of the fact that the negligent act occurred and resulted in harm to the patient
- reduced quality of life
- interest, as above this is not a loss as such but a sum awarded for the delay in receiving the award of general damages from the date that the harm occurred

How damages are calculated

Assessing the amount of damages that should be awarded can be very complex. This is because there are numerous factors that will affect the calculation of the award of damages in specific cases of negligence in healthcare.

With regard to special damages, this will include whether the patient was working prior to the harm being caused, the type of job they had and whether they can still undertake that job, their age and life expectancy and how this affects the anticipated loss of future earnings.

Care and future healthcare costs will be dependent upon the degree of harm that the patient has suffered, and how this limits their ability to undertake daily activities and whether they need to be supported in these activities. If the patient requires further healthcare it will need to be assessed as to how long this will be required for and how extensive the healthcare services will need to be.

There is specific guidance that is used to assess the future care needs for various forms of harm, and to calculate the anticipated costs of these.

As special damages also include an award for future losses and needs, these need to be carefully calculated to ensure that they provide the patient with enough resources to cover all their future losses and needs.

Actuarial tables for different heads of damages are used to make the calculation and are based on such things as the current age of the patient and their life expectancy. Other factors taken into consideration are whether an expense or loss is expected to last for a fixed period of time or for the remainder of the patient's life. Finally, a deduction is made to account for the fact that the

9. DAMAGES

patient in receipt of a lump sum award will be able to obtain an investment return on the damages they have received.

Future losses and care needs are often the most significant part of the overall award of damages.

With regard to general damages, the age and sex of the patient, as well as their previous lifestyle and the nature of the harm they have suffered will all affect the damages they will awarded. The more catastrophic the harm the patient suffers the higher the award will be. Similarly, the site and scope of the injury will affect the head of damages for pain, suffering and loss of amenity.

Whilst it may seem perverse, if a patient has a reduced life expectancy as a consequence of the harm they suffered this could reduce the amount of damages awarded. This is because there is no separate award for the loss of life expectancy as it is not known whether something else would have resulted in the patient dying prematurely, but the reduction in life expectancy means they will have less time to experience the trauma of the harm they have suffered.

As well as the guidance available to assess the cost of a patient's future care costs, there are also guidelines available to assess general damages; these are known as the 'Judicial College Guidelines'. Essentially injuries to any part of the body are assigned a range of financial values to reflect the different ways that the injury may affect different individuals.

The guidelines provide a monetary range for a specific harm based on a number of factors, including:

- the site and severity of the harm
- how long the harm has lasted and is expected to last, if not permanent

- how it affects the patient's daily living
- whether it makes the patient dependant on others
- if it is expected to result in other symptoms
- whether it affects the patient's life expectancy

As examples of the awards in the guidelines

- total blindness and deafness is assessed in the region of £400,000
- acute severe pain ranges from £42,120 to £62,990
- minor brain or head injury ranges from £32,210 to £12,770
- severe brain or head injury ranges from £282,010 to £403,990
- tetraplegia (paralysis affecting arms and legs) is on the range £24,600 to £403,990
- minor injury with recovery in 7 days or less has a maximum of £690
- though if the recovery of a minor injury lasts up to 28 days the award increases to £1,290
- Female infertility is in the range £114,900 to £170,280

The amount of damages within the guidelines is periodically reviewed and updated. It has to be remembered that these are the figures for the award of general damages and do not take into account any of the heads of damage under special damages. So the amount of the full award of damages will be higher.

In short: special damages + general damages (and any punitive award) = total award of damages.

When all the various heads of damages are taken into account in making an award of damages, it can be seen why an award of damages may be extremely high. However, it has to be remembered that the award of damages has to last for the life of the patient and cover all their future needs.

9. DAMAGES

The apparent high value of damages awarded is one reason why it was stated in chapter 4 that vicarious liability and indemnity insurance should be seen as an advantage for patients making claims of negligence in healthcare. As it means that it is the healthcare practitioner's employer or indemnity provider who will fund the award of damages. It is hard to see most healthcare practitioners being able to fund an award of damages for a catastrophic brain injury.

When damages may be reduced

The principle of awarding damages in cases of negligence in healthcare is to put the patient back in the position they would have been in had the harm not occurred and to recognise that the harm has occurred. A patient who has been a victim of negligence in healthcare is not supposed to gain an advantage as a consequence. Therefore, there are ways in which the award of special damages can be reduced to prevent the patient from receiving a financial advantage.

General damages are not affected by this section as they are not seen as providing a financial advantage to the patient.

Contributory negligence

The first way in which damages may be reduced was discussed in chapter 8, when we considered patients who contribute to their own harm. In chapter 8 it was noted that contributory negligence occurs where the patient making the claim of negligence in healthcare is said to have contributed to the harm they have suffered.

It was also noted that the effect of a patient being found to have contributed to their own harm will be to have the amount of damages they would otherwise receive reduced by a sum proportionate to their contribution to the overall negligence.

Thus, if a patient were to have received an award of damages of £100,000 but was found to be 30% contributory negligent, the actual award of damages they would receive would be £70,000.

Costs of making a claim

It is possible, but unusual, that the award of damages will not include a head of damages for the patient's legal costs, or that the damages for this do not cover the full amount of the fees. In either of these situations the patient would need to fund the legal costs that are outstanding themselves, usually from the award of damages.

Interim payments

Sometimes a patient making a claim for negligence in healthcare will receive an interim payment of damages, for example to allow them to make adjustments to their home. If an interim payment is made the value of this will be deducted from the payment made as the final award of damages.

State benefits

Whilst waiting for a claim for negligence in healthcare to be decided, a patient may need to claim certain state benefits, if, for instance, they are no longer able to work or they need someone to care for them. Certain benefits that are paid can be recovered from the patient when the award of damages is made. It is usually recovered from the heads of damages relating to past losses as this is where they could be claimed.

The amount that can be reclaimed in respect of state benefits cannot be more than the benefits received and can only be reclaimed for the period between the date of the harm and the date that the award of damages is received or for 5 years, whichever occurs first.

9. DAMAGES

Because the state benefits can only be recovered from the patient, an award of damages may be increased to reflect the fact that the patient will need to repay state benefits they have received.

The benefits which could be affected include:

- attendance allowance
- employment and support allowance
- housing benefit
- income support
- invalidity allowance
- jobseeker's allowance
- sickness benefit
- unemployment benefit
- universal credit

Usually, the recovery of state benefits cannot be taken from general damages or those special damages relating to future losses if the damages received relating to past losses does not cover the amount of state benefits being reclaimed.

Some of the state benefits can only be taken from specific heads of damages. For instance, universal credit and income support can only be recovered if damages are paid for loss of past earnings, and attendance allowance may only be recovered if damages have been awarded for past care costs.

NHS charges

The NHS has a Compensation Recovery Unit (CRU) which seeks to recover the costs of providing NHS care to individuals who are injured in road traffic accidents and also from those who suffer personal injury where a third party was at fault. This means that if a patient were to establish that a healthcare practitioner had been negligent, any NHS costs involved in the care and treatment of the patient from the point of harm to the award of damages would be recoverable.

There are set charges and whenever an award of damages is to be made this has to be reported to the CRU who issue a certificate detailing the amount that has to be paid.

The amount that needs to be paid has to be paid by the defendant. Thus, it is does not come out of the award of damages but is an additional amount on top of the award of damages that is paid on behalf of the patient. As an example, if a patient were awarded total damages of £1,000,00 and the CRU certificate stated that £50,000 needed to be paid to the NHS, the patient would receive the full £1,000,00 and the defendant would pay an additional £50,000 to the CRU.

It is also the CRU which deals with the recovery of state benefits.

Summary of chapter 9

Damages are paid on the successful conclusion of a claim of negligence in healthcare by a patient. They are usually made as a once and for all payment to the patient and cover all past losses and future losses the patient will incur, as well as a payment in recognition of the fact that the negligent act happened at all.

Because the award of damages has to last for the lifetime of the patient, the amount of damages has to be carefully calculated so that it does not run out. There are specific guidelines and actuarial tables that assist in the calculation of the final amount of damages a patient will receive. Although the actual award of damages can be reduced if the patient has been judged to contribute to their own harm, and in respect of certain payments the patient may have received.

CHAPTER 10

REVISITING THE MILK FLOAT

As the final chapter, chapter 10 revisits the analogy we have used to discuss negligence in healthcare, that of the milk float. After this revisit of the milk float, chapter 10 moves on to examine why a patient chooses to drive a milk float, that is the reasons why patients make a claim of negligence in healthcare against healthcare practitioners. This leads into a discussion of the alternatives to milk floats, or the alternatives to pursuing a legal claim that are available to patients.

The financial cost of milk floats, that is the financial cost of negligence in healthcare within the National Health Service is explored before considering how a milk float is driven or the process of making a claim for negligence in healthcare.

Chapter 10 ends by looking at the effects of the milk float on its driver and those it drives past, that is the effects of negligence in healthcare.

The milk float revisited

Chapter 1 introduced the milk float as an analogy for discussing negligence in healthcare. It was stated that the milk float analogy works as follows, (with the addition of the chapters where the specific part of the milk float is discussed):

- milk floats move slowly and are incapable of moving fast – the same as the civil legal process where negligence in healthcare is dealt with (chapter 2)
- there is a steering wheel that is used to set the direction of travel – a legal case involving negligence is driven to determine whether there was any fault (chapter 10)
- milk floats have four wheels (originally they had three but thankfully there was an increase to four, or the analogy would not work!) – there are four things that need to be determined to prove a case of negligence (chapter 3)
- wheel 1 = duty of care (chapter 4)
- wheel 2 = was there a breach of the duty? (chapter 5)
- wheel 3 = did any harm occur? (chapter 6)
- wheel 4 = did the breach cause the harm? (chapter 7)
- the spare wheel = time – there are limitations on when a case for negligence can be brought (chapter 8)
- applying the brake stops the milk float going forward, this is the same as raising a valid defence (chapter 8)
- milk floats carry milk, in crates. When they leave the milk depot the crates contain bottles full of milk and when they come back they are full of empty bottles. The amount of milk being carried = the amount of damages that are awarded (chapter 9)
- if a wheel comes off the milk float, all the milk moves around and can come off the milk float. If one of the things that the wheels represent is not proved the case is lost, and no damages are paid, similar to the milk being lost. Additionally, there is only a limited supply of milk that can be carried and this equates to the total amount of damages that can be claimed or received (chapters 4–9).
- as well as milk being carried, milk floats also carry non-milk products, this is similar to the two types of damages that may be payable – general and special damages (chapter 9)

10. REVISITING THE MILK FLOAT

The main purpose of a milk float is to deliver milk to customers. The main purpose of making a claim of negligence in healthcare is to obtain a monetary award (damages) for the patient and thus help restore them to the position they would have been in had the harm not occurred, or to assist them with the adjustments to their life they need to make as a consequence of that harm.

To make a successful claim of negligence in healthcare by a healthcare practitioner a patient needs to prove that: the healthcare practitioner owed them a duty of care (chapter 4 examined the duty of care that a healthcare practitioner owes to their patients); that this duty of care was breached by the healthcare practitioner failing to meet the required standard of care (chapter 5 discussed the standard of care and the legal test to determine how a breach of the standard is established); that the patient suffered harm (chapter 6 considered what constitutes harm); that the harm they suffered was caused by the healthcare practitioner's breach of the duty of care (chapter 7 examined causation and the two legal tests which determine whether harm can be said to have occurred as a result of the breach of the standard of care); and that the healthcare practitioner does not have a lawful defence for their actions or omissions or to the claim itself (chapter 8 outlined the various defences that are available to a healthcare practitioner in relation to their actions or omissions, and to the claim itself).

The outcome of a successful claim by a patient will be the award of damages, as discussed in chapter 9.

Milk float deliveries and making a claim of negligence in healthcare

This section considers why a patient may pursue a legal claim of negligence in healthcare. However, before looking at the motivation behind someone making a claim of negligence in healthcare, this section will firstly discuss trivial and fraudulent claims.

Frivolous and fraudulent claims

It is often reported that society is becoming increasingly litigious and that the United Kingdom is moving toward the United States of America in this regard and, as a consequence, a culture of expecting to be compensated for the most trivial of events has now become the norm.

In some ways this can be seen in the many 'stories' of patients who have tried to sue a healthcare practitioner or a healthcare organisation for what many people would not even register as an event. Whilst some seem apocryphal, unfortunately many are not and point to the frivolous nature of some 'legal claims' that are made.

We are not suggesting that just because one person does not give the same gravity to what another regards as important to them means that the event is trivial or frivolous. Rather we are saying that every person has the right to draw attention to what has happened to them, but that there are some individuals who believe that they should receive compensation for what could be called an inconvenience rather than harm as we have discussed it throughout this book.

For instance, we are personally aware of patients alleging negligence in healthcare for the following, and threatening legal action if they do not receive 'compensation':

- being served cold food instead of a hot meal as an inpatient
- a hot meal being cold when the patient came to eat it
- the pain caused when a sticking plaster was removed, same for sutures and wound dressings, when there is no damage to the skin

10. REVISITING THE MILK FLOAT

- being called by the wrong name
- not having access to a television to watch the last episode of a TV series
- being treated by someone else because their usual healthcare practitioner was off duty
- not being able to book a specific day for an operation and therefore missing an important event
- a relative who alleged negligence because they could not smoke a cigarette in an intensive care unit when visiting their spouse, 'to calm their nerves'

It has to be said none of these 'claims' involved any lawyers, and it appeared as if the 'claimant' was just 'trying their luck'. Needless to say, none of these resulted in any award being made to the 'claimant'.

Then there are the reports that can be read in the media, on what seems to be a regular basis, of individuals who have made what appears to be a justified and reasonable claim for significant harm they have suffered due to the negligence of a healthcare practitioner, but are in fact fraudulent in some way.

There are two ways a fraudulent claim can be made. Either the 'claimant' makes up the harm in its entirety, for instance saying that their mobility has been significantly limited and has a major impact on their daily life, when in fact their mobility is unaffected. Alternately, the claimant can grossly exaggerate the extent of the harm they have suffered, for instance stating that they can only walk 10 yards unaided or can only stand for 10 minutes, when they are able to do either of these for much longer, but not as much as they could before the harm occurred.

If a person were found to have submitted a fraudulent claim they can be prosecuted for the criminal offence of fraud or held in contempt of court.

It is also possible for a civil restraint order to be issued where multiple claims are made without merit by an individual.

Motivation of patients who pursue legal claims

We have noted in this chapter that the outcome of a successful claim of negligence in healthcare by a patient will be the award of damages. For many patients this will be their primary motivation or need in making their claim. They have suffered considerable harm, and they need the money to be able to adapt their lives to cope with that harm or because they are now unable to work.

However, even for those whose primary aim is financial, there is often not a single reason that leads to a patient deciding to make a claim of negligence in healthcare against a healthcare practitioner. Patients are typically motivated by a combination of reasons.

Whilst it is outside the scope of this book to provide a detailed analysis of the motivations of patients who do decide to pursue a negligence in healthcare, it is possible to highlight some of the reasons that have been said by patients to have motivated them to pursue a claim.

These motivations include:

- a desire for justice
- to find out what happened to them and why it happened
- to hold someone accountable for what happened/because no-one is taking accountability for what happened to them
- because the procedures for making a complaint are unclear or not navigable to them/has not provided them with what they want/need
- they have not received the outcome they wanted from a complaint or other route or raising their concerns
- to obtain a financial settlement

10. REVISITING THE MILK FLOAT

- because of concerns about the poor practice of a healthcare practitioner(s)
- to raise a safety concern
- to receive an apology
- because the apology they received is not enough/is not considered to be sincere
- for emotional closure over the event
- to ensure that what happened to them does not happen to others by bringing attention to it
- to encourage others to do the same
- to share their experiences
- because the organisation they complained to is not treating their complaint seriously/or is not treating them appropriately, for instance being condescending in their communication
- to blame someone for the harm they have suffered
- to change clinical practice
- to have the validity of their experiences recognised

It has been acknowledged that the outcome for the patient who is successful in their claim of negligence in healthcare is the award of damages, that is an amount of money paid to them. Thus, for many of the motivations listed above pursuing a claim of negligence in healthcare against a healthcare practitioner will not achieve what the patient wants.

This leads us to consider alternatives to pursuing a legal claim, which is discussed in the next section.

Alternatives to making a legal claim of negligence in healthcare

This section is concerned with the alternatives to making a claim of negligence in healthcare for patients who have suffered harm. The aim of this section is not to demean or belittle the motivation behind someone's claim by suggesting that they are wrong to pursue a claim of negligence in healthcare. Rather it is to highlight that they may not get the result they want by pursuing a claim of negligence in healthcare and how this could be achieved, either instead of a negligence in healthcare claim, or in addition to it where the financial element is needed.

There are several alternatives to litigation and whether they are appropriate for a patient is dependent upon the outcome that the patient is seeking. Although if the patient is seeking a financial outcome they will need to pursue a claim of negligence in healthcare. Some of the alternatives discussed below can be used at the same time as issuing a claim of negligence in healthcare, such as making a complaint, whilst others can be used as a way of settling a claim for negligence in healthcare, such as alternative dispute resolution.

What follows are suggestions of where the motivations for patients making a claim of negligence in healthcare can be addressed, based on the list of motivations in the previous section. These are just our suggestions and other commentators may have different opinions of the outcomes that could be achieved for each of them.

Complaints

All healthcare organisations are required to have a complaints process. In addition, for NHS patients there are national complaints processes in each of the four nations of the United Kingdom.

Complaints processes are designed to ensure that the quality of service is maintained and that issues raised by patients are addressed, as well as assisting in the improvement of services.

10. REVISITING THE MILK FLOAT

If a patient is seen outside of the NHS there will be a separate independent complaints process, but if the patient is one who the NHS has sent to an independent hospital or healthcare facility, then the patient should also be able to use the NHS complaints system.

Using a complaints process may assist a patient with:

- finding out what happened to them and why it happened
- raising concerns about the poor practice of a healthcare practitioner(s)
- raising a safety concern
- receiving an apology
- ensuring that what happened to them does not happen to others by bringing attention to it
- blaming someone for the harm they have suffered
- changing clinical practice
- having the validity of their experiences recognised
- holding someone accountable for what happened, although no action may be taken against an individual healthcare practitioner

The Parliamentary and Health Service Ombudsman

This is an independent organisation which has the power to investigate complaints about the NHS in England. They also produce reports which details the cases they have investigated and on areas of specific concern and the quality of NHS services.

To raise a complaint with the Parliamentary and Health Service Ombudsman a patient first needs to have raised a complaint with an NHS organisation. Thus, the Parliamentary and Health Service Ombudsman is a mechanism for having a complaint reviewed and adjudicated.

Decisions made by the Parliamentary and Health Service Ombudsman are open to review by the High Court as a last resort.

Using the Parliamentary and Health Service Ombudsman may assist a patient with:

- holding someone accountable for what happened/because no-one is taking accountability for what happened to them
- procedures for making a complaint that are unclear or not navigable to them/ or where the outcome of the complaint has not provided them with what they want/need
- not receiving the outcome they wanted from a complaint or other route or raising their concerns
- raising a safety concern
- an apology they received that is not enough/is not considered to be sincere
- ensuring that what happened to them does not happen to others by bringing attention to it
- having the validity of their experiences recognised
- the organisation they complained to not treating their complaint seriously/or is not treating them appropriately, for instance being condescending in their communication
- changing clinical practice

Patient associations/support organisations

There are various patient organisations that exist solely to support patients with particular conditions and to campaign for improvements in services for those conditions, or to highlight awareness of the condition. Some organisations also offer support to patients who have been a victim of negligence in healthcare.

10. REVISITING THE MILK FLOAT

There are other organisations which are not solely health related but also offer support to individuals, for instance assistance with making a complaint or pursuing legal action.

Patient support organisations may assist a patient with:

- emotional closure over the event
- sharing their experiences
- encouraging others to do the same
- having the validity of their experiences recognised

Healthcare regulatory bodies

Healthcare regulatory bodies were discussed in chapter 4 where it was noted that one of their functions is to ensure that the public is protected from incompetent healthcare practitioners.

A patient may make a complaint to a healthcare regulatory body about a healthcare practitioner if the practitioner is registered with that healthcare regulatory body. There are healthcare regulatory bodies for the different healthcare practitioner occupational groups, which body regulates which occupational group is discussed in chapter 4.

It is only possible to raise a concern about a healthcare practitioner and not about healthcare in general with a healthcare regulatory body. Therefore they may assist a patient with:

- finding out what happened to them and why it happened
- a desire for justice
- holding someone accountable for what happened/where no-one is taking accountability for what happened to them
- concerns about the poor practice of a healthcare practitioner(s)
- ensuring that what happened to them does not happen to others by bringing attention to it

- blaming someone for the harm they have suffered
- having the validity of their experiences recognised

Alternative dispute resolution

As the name suggests alternative dispute resolution (ADR) is an alternative to taking legal action. It is designed to settle an issue outside of the court process. It is meant to be cheaper and faster than taking legal action.

There are four main types of ADR:

- arbitration
- conciliation
- mediation
- referral to an ombudsman

The healthcare ombudsman is discussed above and cannot assist with claims of negligence in healthcare, but may be able to help with the other motivations as noted above, and won't be discussed any further here.

There are similarities between the various forms of ADR. The main differences between them are:

- arbitration involves an arbitrator who is independent from either side and will make a decision about the issue being complained about. The decision of the arbitrator is legally binding which means it would not be possible to pursue legal action if the decision is not what someone wanted
- conciliation utilises a conciliator who will listen to the issues of both sides and try to reach an agreed solution between both sides that each is happy with
- meditation uses a mediator who will assist each side to consider what it is they want as an outcome and then find common ground and assist each side to move toward

10. REVISITING THE MILK FLOAT

a solution to the issue. The mediator does not make a decision but assists the sides in reaching a common decision/outcome

In cases of negligence in healthcare mediation is the method of ADR used. It can be quite a lengthy process, often over a number of days, and involves the patient and their legal representatives and the defendant and/or their legal representatives. Whilst mediation is not compulsory in claims of negligence in healthcare, if it is not used the Court may require an explanation by one or both sides as to why it has not been attempted.

Mediation is often said to be an alternative to litigation. The mediator has the power to settle the claim if possible, though this requires both sides to agree to the details of the settlement.

Briefly, the mediation process works as follows:

- there is an introductory session from the mediator explaining the process and what to expect, as well as clarifying the issue
- each side will give a presentation of the issue from their perspective
- the mediator will have private sessions with each side to determine what is important to them and what they may be willing to give ground on
- the mediator will go back and forth between private sessions to try to narrow the ground between both sides and reach a settlement, where possible – this part of the process has been referred to as shuttlecock diplomacy
- both sides will be brought back together
- the outcome or settlement will be agreed by both sides, where possible

The differences between litigation and mediation are:

NEGLIGENCE IN HEALTHCARE

Litigation	Mediation
adversarial	non-adversarial
no co-operation	the two sides need to co-operate
each side works independently	can influence each other through the mediator
Judge decides the outcome	It is the parties involved that decide the outcome
Binding outcome	Outcome is not binding unless both sides agree to it
Rigid rules concerning evidence etc	structured informal process
Expensive	Less expensive
Legal rules decide the issue	Issue to be resolved is decided by both sides
Judge is there to rule on disputes	Mediator is there to overcome issues by mediating with both sides

Alternative dispute resolution may assist a patient with:

- finding out what happened to them and why it happened
- where the procedures for making a complaint are unclear or not navigable to them/has not provided them with what they want/need
- receiving the outcome they wanted from a complaint or other route or raising their concerns
- receiving an apology
- having their complaint treated seriously and appropriately
- having the validity of their experiences recognised
- achieving justice

10. REVISITING THE MILK FLOAT

Final point and resources

If a patient needs to receive a financial settlement because they have suffered considerable harm, and they need the money to be able to adapt their lives to cope with that harm or because they are now unable to work, they will need to pursue a claim of negligence in healthcare. The alternatives listed in this section will not be able to provide that. ADR will only result in a financial settlement if it undertaken as part of an initial claim of negligence in healthcare.

The purpose of pursuing the alternative methods discussed is to achieve an outcome in relation to the non-financial motivations of making a claim of negligence in healthcare.

We have listed the details of some organisations that provide assistance with alternatives to making a claim of negligence in healthcare in the resources section, and also those organisations who can act on a complaint or concern.

The financial cost of negligence in healthcare

This section examines the financial cost to the NHS associated with defending and settling claims of negligence in healthcare. It also provides detail on the number of claims in a given year and how many went to court.

It is important to remember that the costs of claims of negligence in healthcare to the NHS come out of the public purse. It is money that could be used for other NHS purposes.

In the information that follows, the details relating to 2022–23 come from the NHS Resolution Annual Reports and Accounts 22/23.

In 1993 £125,000,000 was paid in relation to claims of negligence in healthcare.

NEGLIGENCE IN HEALTHCARE

In 2003 this figure was £446,000,000

In 2013 this had risen to £1,280,000,000.

According to the latest annual report from NHS resolution, the NHS body that deals with claims of negligence in healthcare, for the year 2022–23 the figure was £2,690,900,000.

The amount estimated to be needed to pay all existing claims is £69,614,000,000.

There were 13,511 new claims of negligence in healthcare in 2022–23.

Obstetrics is the area of healthcare that had the most claims in 2022–23 with 1,392 claims made, followed by emergency medicine with 1,292 claims, and then orthopaedic surgery with 1,127 claims.

Of the total amount paid in relation to claims of negligence in healthcare in 2022–23, 57% accounted for damages paid to claimants, with the remaining 43% being the costs, both defence and claimant costs, associated with the claims.

It is often said that 80% of costs associated with negligence in healthcare arise from only 20% of claims.

In 2022–23 80% of claims were settled without court proceedings. Therefore only 20% of cases had court proceedings issued, meaning that the patient has notified the court of their claim and let the defendant know that they intend to take them to court and have a judge give a verdict.

Only 0.19% of cases actually went to court to receive a judgment in 2022–23, of which approximately 37% resulted in damages being awarded.

10. REVISITING THE MILK FLOAT

The process of making a claim of negligence in healthcare

This section discusses the process of making a claim of negligence in healthcare.

Making a claim for negligence in healthcare is complex, slow and subject to numerous rules and procedures, including time limits, all of which have to be complied with in a particular order. Failure to do so could result in the claim not proceeding.

What follows is not a detailed analysis of the process of issuing and serving a claim of negligence in healthcare. That could, and indeed does, fill a book on its own. Rather, it is a brief outline of the main steps in a typical general claim to act as an illustration of the process from the patient's perspective.

- Patient suffers harm
- Patient writes to the hospital and seeks an explanation, this may be through the hospital's complaints procedure
- Hospital will investigate and respond to patient
- At this point if patient is satisfied they may decide to end the matter. If they are not satisfied the process continues
- Patient contacts a solicitor and discusses their case and options with them
- Funding will need to be discussed – options are:
    - Patient pays – self funded, if successful can reclaim costs
    - Conditional fee or 'no win no fee' arrangements – no costs are payable if the case is unsuccessful but as well as receiving the costs paid by the defendants, the patient's solicitor may also deduct costs from the damages awarded
    - Legal expenses insurance is included in some home

insurance policies and with some trade union memberships
- Legal aid is only available for children born with severe brain injury or it occurs as a result of negligence within eight weeks of their birth
- Patient's solicitor will request a copy of patient's healthcare records
- Patient's solicitor will instruct an expert to review the healthcare records and advise whether there is a viable claim, which will include a valuation of the claim
- The expert may decide that there is no real prospect of the claim being successful
- If it is decided that the case is viable, the patient's solicitor will prepare a letter of claim that is sent to the defendant's solicitors. This is the formal notification that details the basis for the patient's claim, as well the evidence to support the claim, and details of what they are seeking, that is the amount of damages
- The defendant, and their solicitors, have 14 days to acknowledge receipt and three months to provide a full response to the letter of claim, the reply is known as a letter of response
- The letter of response will outline the defendant's position, and will include their own evidence with the possible addition of evidence from their own expert. The letter of response will also set out what of the patient's claim they agree with and what they do not agree with. The defendant may then refute the claim; offer to settle with no liability; or offer to settle admitting liability
- It is possible that on receipt of the letter of response the patient will decide not to proceed any further with their claim

10. REVISITING THE MILK FLOAT

- If there is an offer to settle this will be reviewed by the patient and their solicitor, if it is acceptable then the claim can be settled at that point. If it is insufficient the patient's solicitor may negotiate with the defendant's solicitor to try to secure a higher settlement payment
- If the defendant's refute the claim or the settlement amount is insufficient after any negotiation, the claim may proceed to court
- To proceed to court the patient's solicitor will file a claim form and particulars of claim with the court, this is known as issuing proceedings, and the claim form will be stamped by the court with a date. The claim form will outline the details of the claim and the amount of damages being sought
- Then the claim form and particulars of claim need to be served on the defendant, this means that it is sent to the defendant
- The patient's solicitor then prepare for trial, including appointing a barrister to represent the patient at court
- If the case goes to trial the evidence will be presented, including that of witnesses, and this will involve cross examination by the opposing side. There will also be a closing argument by both sides. The judge will then give their judgment

There is no guarantee that a patient will be successful at any stage of the claims process. If we recall the four wheels of the milk float, just because harm has occurred does not mean that damages will be paid to the patient. Negligence has to be proved.

It must be remembered that most claims do not proceed to the court stages, although if they do then the costs of the claim rise substantially due to the cost of specialist solicitors, barristers and expert witnesses' fees.

It is possible to pursue a claim for negligence in healthcare without the assistance of lawyers, known as acting as a litigant in person. This is generally not advised as the process is detailed and complex and failing to comply with it can result in the defendant requesting the court to 'strike out' the claim. Striking out being the legal term for throwing the case out.

As stated in chapter 9, the costs of bringing the claim are usually paid by the losing side, who will therefore pay for the costs of both sides.

A claim of negligence in healthcare is a lengthy process. Every case is different, but it can take up to a year to be in a position to be ready to send the letter of claim to the defendant's solicitor. The defendant then has three months to send their letter of response.

Negotiations regarding a settlement can vary from a month or two to a year or more. Then, if the claim proceeds to court it would not be unusual to wait for two or more years for the claim to be heard.

Consequences of negligence in healthcare

This final section considers the effects that negligence in healthcare can have on the individuals involved and the wider provision and practice of healthcare. It is not meant to be an in-depth review of the effects and consequences of negligence in healthcare upon the participants in claims of negligence in healthcare, the claimants and defendants, or as we know them, patients and healthcare practitioners. We are both aware that there have been substantial research studies that have undertaken this. Rather it is an acknowledgment that a claim of negligence in healthcare affects those involved.

10. REVISITING THE MILK FLOAT

Effects on those involved in a claim

The previous section, on making a claim of negligence in healthcare, presented a matter of fact description of the process of making a claim. We intended it to be that way, to remove the emotion from the process and to make it simpler. However, no claim of negligence in healthcare progresses without emotions.

The reason that emotions are involved is that there are individuals involved in a claim of negligence in healthcare. It is easy to forget this when discussing the finer legal points of a negligence in healthcare claim and what has to be proved for a claim to be successful.

If we return to the purpose of negligence in healthcare as stated in chapter 3, it was to compensate someone for the harm they have suffered as a result of the negligence that occurred during their care and treatment. This means that an individual, the patient, has suffered harm and another person, the healthcare practitioner, is being blamed for that harm and been asked to account for it and remedy it.

Negligence in healthcare has a cost greater than any money involved. The fact that they have suffered harm is going to have emotional effects on the patient. Likewise, knowing that they may have caused harm to a patient will emotionally affect the healthcare practitioner, as will the possibility that their career will be affected. For both patient and healthcare practitioner there is anxiety and stress related to the event but also to the process of the claim and how it is resolved. Neither knows what the outcome will be when the process of making a claim is started, this uncertainty only adds to the emotional toil.

We are not saying that either of these emotional responses is more important than the other, for we are simply noting that both patient and healthcare practitioner are affected and that here are two parties involved in every claim of negligence in healthcare.

Effects on those not involved in a claim

Negligence in healthcare can also be said to have an effect on individuals who are in no way related to an actual claim.

It is right that patients receive damages for the harm they have suffered but it needs to be remembered that just because a mistake happens it does not mean that a healthcare practitioner has been negligent. As stated in chapter 1, negligence is a way of determining if a healthcare practitioner's standard of care and/or treatment has been below standard. It is possible for a healthcare practitioner to practise at the required standard but for the patient to suffer an unavoidable and unforeseeable consequence of their treatment.

Additionally, there are also systems failures such as administrative errors resulting in patient data being missing, these can lead to delays in patients receiving the necessary care and treatment.

The reporting on the increase in the number of claims being made of negligence in healthcare and the associated costs of this can also have an adverse effect on healthcare practitioners and their practice.

For instance, there are reports in healthcare practitioner journals and in the national media about defensive practice by healthcare practitioners to lessen the risk of them facing a claim of negligence in healthcare. Defensive practice is when a healthcare practitioner does not provide individualised patient care and treatment but provides the care and treatment according to set protocols and policies. This can result in patients receiving unnecessary tests and investigations and their treatment being delayed. It can also mean that a patient receives a simper treatment listed in the protocol over a more complex treatment that may be more effective for that patient.

10. REVISITING THE MILK FLOAT

In addition, reports of negligence in healthcare can erode the trust and confidence that patients have in their healthcare practitioners, in contrast there may be patients that have an unrealistic perception of what healthcare practice can achieve. For either type of patient, if something goes wrong it has to be someone's fault.

With regard to the actual claim of negligence in healthcare, it has to be remembered that it is the patient who has to prove their case. The healthcare practitioner does not have to prove their defence. If the patient is unsuccessful in proving their case the healthcare practitioner is successful and the patient will not receive any remedy for their harm.

This has led to calls for a 'no fault' compensation scheme to be introduced to manage incidents where patients are harmed. Such a system has operated in New Zealand since 1974. In essence a patient can receive compensation without having to prove that any particular individua or organisation was at fault. In some ways it can be likened to an extension of the res ipsa loquitur principle discussed in chapter 7. The fact that the patient has suffered harm is sufficient to justify awarding them compensation.

The New Zealand scheme is said to be quicker and cheaper as there is less need for legal argument. The main issue involved is the amount of compensation that is needed to restore the patient to the position they had been in. However, if the practice of a healthcare practitioner is considered to be below standard they can still be referred to the relevant healthcare regulatory body.

Effect on healthcare practice

If we remove the individuals from negligence in healthcare and consider the effects that previous claims have had on healthcare practice, negligence can be said to be positive in many regards.

Healthcare practice can be said to have changed considerably over the years. Both of us can testify to that. Some of the ways in which it has changed can be said to be attributable to negligence in healthcare claims, at least in part.

There is a requirement that healthcare practitioners base their practice upon evidence to support their clinical decision making, this is known as evidence based practice and is discussed in chapter 5. In that chapter it was noted that the requirement that a healthcare practitioner's standard of care has a logical basis in the Bolitho v City & Hackney Health Authority [1997] case was a contributory factor to the acceptance of evidence based practice within healthcare.

In turn, that resulted in a requirement that all healthcare practitioners demonstrate that they are up to date in their practice, and can demonstrate that they undertake continuing professional development. Although the best healthcare practitioners have always undertaken evidence based practice and continuing professional development, making it a condition of registration for all healthcare practitioners increases the general standard of practice.

As a consequence of negligence in healthcare claims there is a desire and a will within healthcare to learn from the mistakes that lead to harm and even mistakes that do not lead to harm but have the potential to do so, so-called near misses. This involves the sharing of information, both within and across organisations of what happened, what the cause was and how to address these causes, so that such incidents are not repeated.

All of this has a benefit for patients and healthcare practice alike in ensuring that the quality of healthcare practice is constantly moving and striving towards improvement.

10. REVISITING THE MILK FLOAT

Summary of chapter 10

Chapter 10 revisited the milk float analogy to consider what it is that has to be proved for a patient to make a successful claim of negligence in healthcare, the chapter also discussed the motivations behind patient's making a claim and how a claim is made. It has also discussed various alternatives to making claims of negligence in healthcare that a patient could utilise to meet some of the motivations identified.

The chapter has also identified the cost of negligence in healthcare. Both the financial costs and the effects that claims of negligence in healthcare have on the individuals involved. It ended by considering the wider effects of negligence in healthcare, including some positive effects that can be said to have occurred in healthcare practice.

REFERENCES

Barnett v Chelsea & Kensington Hospital Management Committee [1968] 1 All ER 1068
Blyth v Birmingham Water Works Co. (1856) All ER [1843–60] 478
Bolam v Friern Hospital Management Committee [1957] 2 All ER 118
Bolitho v City & Hackney Health Authority [1997] 4 ALL ER 771
Caparo Industries plc v Dickman and others [1990] 1 All ER 668
Cassidy v Ministry of Health [1951] 2 KB 343
Century Insurance Co. Ltd v Northern Ireland Road Transport Board [1942] 1 ALL ER 491
Cork v Kirby MacLean Ltd [1952] 2 All ER 402
Cornock M & Giddings L (2023) *Healthcare rights and law for patients, carers and practitioners* Straightforward Publishing
Cowley v Cheshire and Merseyside Strategic Health Authority (2007) 94 BMLR 29
Curzon L B (1994) *Dictionary of Law* 4th edition Pitman Publishing, London
Donoghue v Stevenson [1932] All ER 1
F v West Berkshire Health Authority [1989] 2 All ER 545
General Medical Council (2024) *Good medical practice* General Medical Council, London
Goodwill v British Pregnancy Advisory Service [1996] 2 All ER 161
Hall v Brooklands Auto-Racing Club [1932] All ER 208
Health and Care Professions Council (2016) *Standards of conduct, performance and ethics* Health and Care Professions Council, London
Jones v Manchester Corporation [1952] 2 QB 852
Law Reform (Contributory Negligence) Act 1945
Limitation Act 1980
Limpus v London General Omnibus Co. (1863) All ER [1861–73] 556
McFarlane v Tayside Health Board [1999] 4 All ER 961
McKay v Essex Area Health Authority [1982] 2 All ER 771

Maynard v West Midlands Regional Health Authority [1985] 1 All ER 635
Nettleship v Weston [1971] 3 All ER 581
NHS Resolution (2023) *Annual Reports and Accounts 22/23* NHS Resolution, London
Nursing and Midwifery Council (2018) *The Code* Nursing and Midwifery Council, London
Overseas Tankship (U.K.) Ltd v Morts Dock and Engineering Co Ltd [1961] 1 All ER 404
Pearce v United Bristol Healthcare NHS Trust (1998) 48 BMLR 118
Penner J E (2001) *Mozley & Whiteley's Law Dictionary* 12th edition Butterworths, London
R v Adomako [1994] 3 All ER 79
Roe v Ministry of Health [1954] 2 All ER 131
Sackett D, Rosenberg W, Gray J, Haynes R and Richardson W (1996) 'Evidence based medicine: what it is and what it isn't' *British Medical Journal* 312 (7023) p. 71–72
Stevenson A (ed) (2007) *Shorter Oxford English Dictionary* 6th edition Oxford University Press, Oxford
Sutherland Shire Council v Heyman (1985) 60 ALR

GLOSSARY OF NEGLIGENCE RELATED TERMS

Accountability: Being held to account. When a healthcare practitioner has to explain their actions to an employer, their healthcare regulatory body, or to a court of law

Act of Parliament: Also known as statutes, Acts, and primary legislation. They are laws that originate from Parliament or its equivalent, and are written down in one document, known as the Act of Parliament.

Advanced practitioner: A healthcare practitioner who has expanded their role and has skills and expertise above that of the ordinary level of healthcare practitioner in their occupational group.

Balance of probabilities: That one side is more convincing than the other. More likely than not to have happened.

Bolam test: Originally defined in Bolam v Friern Hospital Management Committee [1957] as '*a doctor is not negligent, if he is acting in accordance with a practice accepted as proper by a responsible body of medical men skilled in that particular art*' (at page 118).

The modified 'Bolam test' can be stated as: whether a healthcare practitioner has acted in accordance with practice accepted as proper by a responsible

	body of healthcare practitioners who are skilled in the particular aspect of care or treatment, and that this body of opinion can withstand logical and objective scrutiny.
Breach of duty:	A failure by a healthcare practitioner to meet the duty of care to their patient because they did not achieve the required standard of care.
Burden of proof:	Refers to which party in legal case has to prove their case. In general, in a civil case it is the party which brings the case that has to prove it, and in a criminal case it is the prosecution who has the burden of proving their case.
Carer:	When we use the term carer we are generally thinking of the patient's main non-professional source of support. Although we use this term to mean anyone who supports or cares for, or even provides treatment to a patient but is not paid for their role and does not provide the role because of their job.
Causation:	This is concerned with the relationship between an act and the effect of the act. Asks if the act caused a specific outcome.
Child:	Legally a person under 18. Also known as a minor.
Civil law:	Primarily deals with legal issues between individuals or between companies or organisations or any combination of these
Claimant:	In a civil case, it is the person or organisation who brings the case and who has to prove the case.

GLOSSARY OF NEGLIGENCE RELATED TERMS

Common law:
Refers to law that originates from cases heard in the courts. Relies upon the doctrine of precedent and a hierarchical court system.

Compensation:
Another term for damages paid on successfully bringing a claim for negligence.

Criminal law:
Rules, regulations and legislation concerned with prosecuting those who are said to have breached the criminal law.

Damages:
A sum of money that is designed to put, or attempt to put, the patient in the position they would have been in had the harm not occurred. Will also include any payment for loss and suffering, if appropriate, and to compensate the patient for the fact that the harm occurred.

Comprises general and special damages.

Defendant:
In a case of negligence in healthcare, the individual or organisation that is alleged to have been negligent. The defendant does not have to prove anything and will be successful if the claimant has not proved their case against the defendant. In short, a defendant is the person who the case is against.

Duty:
A legal obligation to do something, or not to do something.

Duty of care:
A legal obligation that one person has to take reasonable care in their interactions with certain other individuals according to a particular set standard.

Expert witness:
Someone appointed to advise the court as to what a reasonable and responsible body of practitioners skilled in the particular

	practice of the defendant healthcare practitioner would have done in the same circumstances.
Foreseeability:	Being able to reasonably predict that a certain action would harm a person affected by the action.
General damages:	Refers to those losses that cannot be accurately calculated.
Good Samaritan:	Someone who voluntarily assists another, usually in an emergency situation.
Harm:	Means any suffering, or physical or psychiatric injury, including death, or any loss, including damage to property, that the patient has experienced.
Healthcare practitioner:	We use this term to mean someone whose occupation is to provide care and treatment to patients. It includes all those who have a role with patients. We are using this term so that we do not need to list each and every type of healthcare practitioner each time we want to discuss something. Examples of healthcare practitioners include chiropodists, dental hygienists and nurses, dieticians, doctors, midwives, nurses, occupational therapists, paramedics, physiotherapists, radiographers, and speech therapists.
	We also use the term to include anyone who is a student training to be a healthcare practitioner.
Indemnity:	A form of insurance policy which is designed to provide assistance in the event that the policyholder faces certain events, such as being sued for negligence in healthcare.

GLOSSARY OF NEGLIGENCE RELATED TERMS

	Most healthcare practitioners, those in employment by the National Health Service for instance, will have their indemnity through the vicarious liability of their employer for their actions.
Law:	A rule that is considered to be so important that it has been given special meaning and has a penalty attached to it, which can be applied if the law is not followed. The aim of the penalty being to encourage us all to abide by the law.
Legal jurisdiction:	A legally established geographical area. Essentially, a country that has its own legal system and is able to make its own laws. There are four separate jurisdictions in the United Kingdom. These are England, Northern Ireland, Scotland, and Wales. Some laws cover the whole of the United Kingdom, some only apply to one jurisdiction and others apply to two or more jurisdictions.
Legal person:	An actual person or a legally constructed entity, such as an organisation or a company, that is able to face a legal challenge in court or to bring a legal case against another legal person.
Legislation:	There are several terms used to describe legislation, these include statutes, Acts, primary legislation, and secondary legislation. Whatever term is used, in the United Kingdom they refer to law that is made in the Westminster Parliament, or the Scottish Parliament, or the Northern Ireland Assembly or the Welsh Senedd. Whilst the Westminster Parliament can

	pass laws that affect the whole of the United Kingdom, the laws made in the other three law making institutions only have effect in their respective countries.
Liability:	Being held to account, but with the additional burden that if the account given is not satisfactory a penalty may be imposed.
Limitation period:	The requirement that legal proceedings are started with a given period of time of the event occurring.
Milk float:	The slow electric vehicles that were used to deliver milk to the front doors of an individual customer's house early each morning. Nowadays the vehicles tend to be petrol or diesel powered and as a result are a lot faster.
Negligence:	Breaching a duty of care so that it results in harm to someone.
	It is a form of tort that attempts where possible to put individuals in the position they would have been in had a specific wrong not occurred. The result of a successful action in tort can result in individuals receiving an award of damages for the wrong that has happened to them.
Negligence in healthcare:	Negligence that occurs during the care and treatment of a patient, or when a patient should be receiving care and/or treatment but doesn't, so that the healthcare practitioner's duty of care to the patient is breached resulting in harm to the patient. Also known as clinical negligence.

GLOSSARY OF NEGLIGENCE RELATED TERMS

Neighbour principle: A person owes a duty of care to those who could reasonably be said to be affected by their actions.

Non-pecuniary Non-financial losses and harm suffered by a claimant.

Novus actus interveniens: Literally 'a new act intervenes'. Means that causation cannot be actually proved if a new act breaks the chain of causation from the original negligent act by the healthcare practitioner to the harm suffered by the patient.

Patient: We use this to mean someone who is interacting with healthcare practitioners and may be receiving healthcare and/or treatment or expecting to receive care and/or treatment. We use the term patient to include client. We also use patient to mean an adult or child.

Pecuniary Financial losses incurred by a claimant.

Plaintiff: Previously used term for what is now the claimant.

Precedent: Refers to a legal doctrine where a judgment made in one case can be used as the basis for the judgment in a later case if the facts and legal issues are similar.

Proximity: Arose as a consequence of the Caparo Industries plc v Dickman and others [1990] case and refers to the closeness of relationship between a claimant and defendant.

Question of fact: Concerned with determining the facts of a case. It asks whether an event happened or whether something met the required level. For instance, it is a question of fact if the four aspects of negligence are proved by the claimant.

Question of law: Concerned with applying the law to the facts of a case and asking what legal remedy is available to correct the wrong, where one has occurred.

Remedy: Putting right or compensating for the harm that has occurred as a result of a tort.

Res ipsa loquitur: 'The thing speaks for itself'. A legal doctrine that can be used to state that it is possible to infer negligence has occurred from the harm that has been suffered.

Special damages: Financial losses that can be accurately calculated.

Standard of care: The level of practice that a healthcare practitioner has to achieve to be deemed to have met their duty of care to their patient.

Standard of proof: This refers to the standard that has to be reached for the prosecution or claimant to be considered to have proved their case.

The standard of proof is different in civil and criminal cases.

In criminal cases the standard is higher than in civil cases and the case has to be proved 'beyond a reasonable doubt'. In reality, this means in all certainty it is considered that X happened, and it is the defendant who was the one who did X.

In civil cases the standard of proof is on the 'balance of probabilities'. In reality,

GLOSSARY OF NEGLIGENCE RELATED TERMS

	this means that a judge is more convinced of one side's account than the other's.
The law:	When we use the term 'the law" we mean the sum total of all the rules that have been given special status (that is, all the individual laws) and the mechanism by which those laws can be enforced.
Tort:	An area of civil law that is concerned with redressing wrongs that have occurred. Gives rise to a claim for damages.
Vicarious liability:	When one person or organisation is liable for the actions of another.
Volenti non fit injuria:	Latin for 'to a willing person, it is not a wrong'. It is a defence in negligence cases where a person voluntarily agrees to a risk of harm which subsequently materialises.

RESOURCES

For patients

Action against Medical Accidents – a charity for patient safety and justice
https://www.avma.org.uk/

Citizens advice
https://www.citizensadvice.org.uk/

Citizens Advice Northern Ireland
https://www.citizensadvice.org.uk/about-us/northern-ireland/

Citizens advice Scotland
https://www.cas.org.uk/

Citizens advice Wales
https://www.citizensadvice.org.uk/about-us/information/advicelink-cymru/

Healthwatch
https://www.healthwatch.co.uk/your-local-healthwatch/list

NHS Complaints advocacy – assists with making a complaint about NHS services
https://www.pohwer.net/nhs-complaints-advocacy

NHS Integrated care Board list
https://www.nhs.uk/nhs-services/find-your-local-integrated-care-board/

NHS Patient Advice and Liaison Service portal– provides assistance with resolving concerns about NHS services
https://www.nhs.uk/nhs-services/hospitals/what-is-pals-patient-advice-and-liaison-service/

RESOURCES

Patient Advice and Liaison Service (PALS)
https://www.nhs.uk/nhs-services/hospitals/what-is-pals-patient-advice-and-liaison-service/

The Advocacy People website – an independent charity which offers support with NHS complaints
https://www.theadvocacypeople.org.uk/

The Patients Association
https://www.patients-assoation.org.uk/making-a-complaint

Support for healthcare practitioners

For those healthcare practitioners who are members of a professional organisation and/or a trade union, we recommend these as a first point of contact

NHS Resolution support for healthcare staff
https://resolution.nhs.uk/services/claims-managemen/support-for-healthcare-staff/

Law and sources of law

How laws are made in Parliament
https://www.gov.uk/guidance/legislative-process-taking-a-bill-through-parliament#:~:text=A%20bill%20is%20a%20proposed,Parliament%20can%20introduce%20a%20bill.

The National Archives United Kingdom legislation website – maintains a searchable website of all current legislation
https://www.legislation.gov.uk/

Crown Prosecutioervice
https://www.cps.gov.uk/

Courts

HM Courts & Tribunals Service website

https://www.gov.uk/government/organisations/hm-courts-and-tribunals-service

Scottish Courts and Tribunals website

https://scotcourts.gov.uk/

Northern Ireland Courts and Tribunals Service website

https://www.justice-ni.gov.uk/topics/courts-and-tribunals

Welsh Courts and Tribunals website

https://law.gov.wales/constitution-and-governmen/administration-justice/courts

Parliament websites

Scottish Parliament website

https://www.parliament.scot/

The Northern Ireland Assembly website

http://www.niassembly.gov.uk/

The Senedd (Welsh Parliament) website

https://senedd.wales/

UK Parliament website

https://www.parliament.uk/

RESOURCES

Ways to raise concerns about healthcare, healthcare practitioners and the legal profession

NHS complaints services

England – https://www.nhs.uk/using-the-nhs/about-the-nhs/how-to-complain-to-the-nhs/

Northern Ireland – https://www.nidirect.gov.uk/articles/raising-concern-or-making-complaint-about-health-services

Scotland – https://www.nhsinform.scot/care-support-and-rights/health-rights/feedback-and-complaints/making-a-complaint-about-your-nhs-care-or-treatment/

Wales – https://www.wales.nhs.uk/ourservices/contactus/nhscomplaints

Websites of the healthcare regulatory bodies

Healthcare Regulatory Body	Website
General Chiropractic Council	https://www.gcc-uk.org/
General Dental Council	https://www.gdc-uk.org/
General Medical Council	https://www.gmc-uk.org/
General Optical Council	https://optical.org/
General Osteopathic Council	https://www.osteopathy.org.uk/home/
General Pharmaceutical Council	https://www.pharmacyregulation.org/
Pharmaceutical Society of Northern Ireland	https://www.psni.org.uk/
Health and Care Professions Council	https://www.hcpc-uk.org/
Nursing and Midwifery Council	https://www.nmc.org.uk/

Bar Standards Board complaints website

https://www.barstandardsboard.org.uk/for-the-public/reporting-concerns.html

Care Quality Commission

https://www.cqc.org.uk/contact-us/how-complain/complain-about-service-or-provider

Parliamentary and Health Service Ombudsman website – can investigate complaints about NHS services which are not resolved through the NHS complaints process

https://www.ombudsman.org.uk/

Professional Standards Authority – has oversight of the healthcare regulatory bodies

https://www.professionalstandards.org.uk/home

The Law Society complaints website

https://www.lawsociety.org.uk/public/for-public-visitors/using-a-solicitor/complain-about-a-solicitor

General

Marc's articles are available to download for free from:

http://oro.open.ac.uk/view/person/mac755.html

INDEX

A

Accident and emergency department, 74, 76
Acting in the course of employment, 84
Advanced Practitioners standard for specialist skills, 137
Aggravated damages, 186
Alternative dispute resolution (ADR), 212, 214
Alternatives to litigation, 208
An intervening act, 176
Arbitration, 212
Assault, 41
Award of damages, 186

B

Battery, 40
Bolam test, 109, 112–118, 120–124, 127, 128, 130–134, 136, 138–141, 143, 175, 229
Breach of duty, 8, 99, 100, 230
Breach of the duty of care, 8, 9, 62, 99, 100, 101, 104, 116, 121, 123, 141, 142, 146, 159, 160, 161, 165, 168, 175, 176, 184, 186, 187, 203
British Pregnancy Advisory Service, 68, 69, 70, 227
Burden of proof, 33, 230

C

Calculating damages, 194
Care costs, 188, 192, 195, 199

Causation, 9, 10, 60, 76, 101, 116, 121, 145, 149, 158–163, 165, 166–170 173, 176, 203, 235
Chain of causation, 10, 158, 176, 235
Civil justice legal system, 28
Common law, 23, 25, 26, 27, 31, 35, 42, 43, 44, 64, 103, 105, 155
Compensation, 165
Compensation Recovery Unit (CRU), 199, 200
Complaints processes, 208
Conciliation, 212
Congenital Disabilities (Civil Liabilities) Act 1976, 149
Contributory negligence, 172, 176, 197
Coroners' Courts, 31
Costs of making a claim, 198
Court of Appeal (Civil Division), 29, 30
Court of Appeal (Criminal Division), 29, 30
Court of Protection, 30
Criminal justice legal system, 28
Criminal Prosecution Service, 32
Crown Court, 29

D

Damage, 185
Damages, 11, 54, 177, 183, 185, 200, 231
Death, 148
Defences in legal cases, 11, 171

Defences available in cases of negligence in healthcare, 172
Definition of negligence, 36, 37
Delegated legislation, 24
Delegation and liability, 92
Department of Health and Social Care, 24
Dispute over the facts, 172, 173
Doctrine of precedent, 26, 27
Duty of care, 8, 61, 62, 63, 72

E

Eggshell skull principle, 10, 158, 169
Emergencies and the standard of care, 131
Emergencies outside a healthcare environment, 133
Evidence based practice, 9, 126, 127, 142, 224
Exemplary damages, 186
Expert witnesses, 9, 32, 99, 115, 116, 117, 118, 121, 219, 231

F

Factual causation, 162
Family Court, 30
False imprisonment, 40
Finding fault, 101
Forms of harm, 147

G

General Chiropractic Council, 79, 241
General damages, 191, 193, 195, 196, 199
General Dental Council, 79, 241
General Medical Council, 79, 80, 96, 227, 241
General Optical Council, 79, 241

General Osteopathic Council, 79, 241
General Pharmaceutical Council, 79, 241
General standard of care, 103
Good Samaritan acts, 8, 61, 93, 94, 95, 96, 98
Gross negligence manslaughter, 10, 28, 145, 155, 156, 157

H

Harm, 9, 145, 185
Heads of damage, 190, 191
Health and Care Professions Council, 79, 96, 227, 241
Healthcare costs, 192, 194
Healthcare regulatory bodies, 211
High Court, 29

I

Indemnity, 88, 89, 232
Injunctions, 42
Interim payments, 198
Intervening acts, 166

J

Judicial College Guidelines, 195

L

Lack of proximity, 68
Law Reform (Contributory Negligence) Act 1945, 177, 227
Legal causation, 167
Legal jurisdictions, 18
Legislation, 24
Liability of healthcare practitioners, 8, 61, 77, 78, 79
Liability of students, 88
Limitation Act 1980 179, 180, 227
Loss of chance, 152

INDEX

Loss of earning capacity, 192
Loss of income, 185, 192, 193
Lump sum payment, 187

M

Magistrates Court, 29
Making a claim of negligence in healthcare, 166, 175, 203, 204, 207, 208, 215, 217, 221
Man on the Clapham omnibus, 105, 106, 107
Material contribution to the harm, 165
Mediation, 212, 213, 214
Milk float and negligence, 13
Milk float and laws, 21
Mistaken identity, 172, 173
Monetary award, 23, 38, 42, 54, 183, 184, 185, 203

N

Negligence before birth, 148, 149
Neighbour principle, 51, 63, 64, 67, 72, 97
Novus actus interveniens, 168, 172, 176
Nurses, 4, 73, 79, 108, 110, 140, 232
Nursing and Midwifery Council, 79, 80, 96, 127, 228, 241
Nuisance, 40

O

One-off lump sum payment, 187, 188
Omission, 160
Ordinary witness, 32

P

Pain and suffering, 152
Paramedics, 5, 79, 108, 232
Parliamentary and Health Service Ombudsman, 209, 210, 242
Patients organizations, 210
Pension loss, 192
Personal injury, 40
Periodical Payment Order, 188, 189
Pharmaceutical Society of Northern Ireland, 79, 241
Physical injury, 149
Physiotherapists, 5, 79, 108, 140, 232
Primary legislation, 24, 229, 233
Primary victim, 151
Proving causation, 159
Proximity and public policy, 70
Psychiatric injury, 150
Punitive damages, 186, 187
Purpose of negligence in healthcare, 53

Q

Quantum, 185

R

Reasonable foreseeability, 66, 67
Reasonable or prudent person test, 105
Reduced life expectancy, 54, 195
Reduced quality of life, 193
Rehabilitation courses, 23
Res ipsa loquitur, 161, 236

S

Secondary legislation, 24, 25, 233
Secondary victim, 151, 157
Self-employed healthcare professionals, 88
Social Action, Responsibility and Heroism Act 2015, 94, 95

245

Special damages, 191, 192, 236
Special relationships, 71
Standard of care, 102, 107, 114, 131, 134
Standards for juniors, 134
Standards for trainees, 134
Standard of proof, 33
State benefits, 198, 199
Statutes, 24, 229, 233
Statutory limitation, 172, 179

T

Team liability, 90
Team standard, 140
Thalidomide, 149
Tort, 39, 43, 52, 237

Trespass, 40
Types of punishment, 23

U

United Kingdom Supreme Court, 28

V

Vicarious liability, 81, 82, 83, 237
Volenti non fit injuria, 172, 178, 237

W

Witnesses, 32
Wrongful birth, 153
Wrongful life, 154

We are not sure why you are still reading, unless you just skipped to the back for a sneak peak of the ending, but we just wanted to say thank you for reading our book, and for purchasing it, if you did that is.

Well, we are off to take the milk float back to the depot.

Thanks,

Marc & Andy